Unleash Your Inner Ultrarunner

Beginner's Guide to Trail Running:
Training for Endurance, Embracing
Epic Outdoor Adventures, and
Conquering Ultra-Distance Racing

Sarah Russell

Table of Contents

Introduction

Did you hear that? The outdoors are calling, inviting you into a world of exquisite beauty and into a life that will transform your physical health and emotional wellbeing. Minute by minute, step by step, mile by mile, you are about to embark on a lifelong adventure that will bring you fitness, confidence, inner strength, friendship, and nature's healing powers. In this comprehensive beginner's guide to the sport of trail running, you will learn how to make the most of your new passion: how best to prepare and train; how to gear up; how to meet the inevitable challenges head-on; and how to remain safe.

Don't be surprised if you find yourself loitering in outdoor equipment stores or suddenly noticing signs in your neighborhood that point to parks and trails. One day soon, you'll walk past a hill and wonder how long it will be before you can run all the way up without stopping. You will suddenly become more aware of how much water you drink and how much protein you consume. When you realize that you are asking everyone you know about their favorite trails, you will realize that you've been lured into one of the most exciting and fulfilling sports ever.

The practical advice and inspirational stories from experienced runners who have contributed to this book will ensure that you are prepared for that first starting line and ready to race across that first finish line with the spirit of a conqueror! There is no doubt that, like so many other runners from all 'walks' of life, you will soon be addicted to the magic of the trail. Happy running!

Chapter 1:

The Trail Beckons: Embracing

a New Adventure

If anyone had asked me 10 years ago if I would ever run 50 miles in one day, I would have laughed. I hated running and was the person who whined and complained every step of the way during the mile run in gym class. Now here I am with five 50-milers, seven 50Ks, and thousands of training miles under my belt. Not only that, but the adventure continues as I look forward to setting new goals and planning my life with training and preparation for the next race in mind!

Understanding the Allure

In his poem "The Joys of the Open Road," poet William Bliss Carman captures the spirit of the trail, rejoicing in the "striding heart from hill to hill" (Carman, 1984). He celebrates the colors and smells of the natural world, the serenity and quiet of the forest, and the healing powers of walking in the outdoors. Carman may not have been a 21st-century trail runner, but he was certainly attuned to the wellness he experienced as he wandered.

In a time when many of us are overworked and stressed (and the couch is so inviting), perhaps we can follow Carman's lead and hit that open road. However, the magic of trail running is even more powerful than simply getting outdoors for a good walk. Much of the magic is in the challenge. Experienced athletes, whether they be runners or those who participate in other sports, know that in order to sustain interest in their fields, they move from physical challenge to physical challenge, forever chasing after that personal record, or PR. For novice athletes, the goal may be weight loss, injury recovery, or gaining a new skill. In every case, though, those who participate in athletics will likely agree that the sense of accomplishment they gain contributes not only to their physical wellbeing but also to their personal growth. Just observe the facial expressions of a runner crossing the finish line, and although you may see exhaustion, you will also see pride, confidence, and joy.

Trail runners, however, experience an additional benefit—a unique, unanticipated gift. They often testify that their time on the trail takes on a meditative or spiritual quality. Focusing solely on the varied and complex terrain immediately in front of them, they find themselves able to leave behind the noise and busyness of their lives and hone in on the messages of the natural world. Many runners report becoming hyperaware of the surrounding details and sharply alert to sounds, smells, sights, and even tastes that they typically do not notice. Trail running is, in a sense, akin to the practice of *Shinrin-yoku*, or forest bathing, which is known to reduce stress hormones, raise moods, boost the immune system, and even induce creativity (MacBride-Stewart, 2019). In fact, it is not unusual to hear that while on the trail, a runner has created the outline for a novel, imagined the tune for a musical composition, or been inspired to paint. This kind of sustained, intense connection with the natural world is not only healing but truly magical. It is no small wonder that, once hooked, we constantly crave a return to the trail.

Breaking Stereotypes: Trail Running for Everyone

Recently, when I was picking up a friend from the hospital, I overheard an elderly gentleman chatting with a nurse as he awaited a very serious surgical procedure. Initially, I felt deep pity for him, as he was obviously in great discomfort, not to mention anxious about the upcoming surgery. I tuned them out for a moment, thinking of how fragile life is and how aging can be such an emotional challenge. Then, however, I perceived a change in his tone. "I'm a runner," he announced to the nurse. "I've completed 32 marathons, many half marathons, 10Ks, 5Ks, even an Iron Man!" The pride in his voice was unmistakable. Then, to my surprise, he added, "I began when I turned 60."

"Wow, impressive!" responded the nurse. "What makes a person want to take on something like that? It's got to be hard on your body."

"If there's a challenge, someone is going to embrace it," he answered. "I did. And I loved every minute of it. You know, some people even run 100K races. If I can handle marathons, I can handle a little cancer."

The two of them went on to discuss his many runs: trail runs in Catalina Island's heat, training runs up and down every neighborhood hill he could find, and slogging through a finish line with mud and rain-soaked shoes. "Those give you blisters," he noted. He beamed as he recalled qualifying for the Boston Marathon. The man's joy was palpable and contagious, and his optimism in the face of disease was heroic.

As the surgical team wheeled him out of the waiting room towards the operating room, he was advising the middle-aged nurse on how she herself could begin training. "You are <u>not</u> too old, but you'll want to begin slowly in order to avoid injury," he suggested. "But eventually, you'll need to run about 30 miles a week. Pick some pretty trails. You will love it."

I smiled to myself as I realized that any sense of pity I had for this charismatic man had dissipated in the presence of his resilience.

Age Considerations

If you chat with a variety of runners about their histories, you will quickly discover a diversity of stories. Some begin the sport as children, often following in the footsteps of their parents or grandparents. Many runners begin in middle or high school when they join their school's cross-country team. Perhaps most surprisingly, others begin their running careers later in life, like the gentleman in the hospital. Any running coach will emphasize that there is no age limit, just physical and emotional challenges to overcome, no matter what the age.

As with any sport, the serious trail or road runner should consult with medical professionals during their annual physical to ensure that training is planned appropriately and with risk avoidance in mind. The nutritional needs of a growing 12-year-old are very different from those of a 63-year-old. A younger individual and a "grandmaster" over 60 will benefit from different strength training and stretching routines. Many runners also consult kinesiologists, sports medicine doctors, or physical therapists when developing a training plan or recovering from a sports injury.

Children

One of the delights I frequently encounter on a morning training run is passing a parent with an infant in a carrier backpack or with a toddler riding in a hiking stroller. Inevitably, both parent and child are grinning. This is no surprise, as children are inherently fascinated by the natural world, and a jaunt outdoors always relieves the stresses that today's parents experience.

The deeper beauty of these moments, however, is future-oriented. Family adventures on the trail are bound to prepare that child for an adult life of good health, exercise, and appreciation of the outdoor environment. Many professional runners, both on the road and on the trail, inherit their passion from their families and will likely pass it on to the next generation. Even the trail "walkers," who simply enjoy a relaxed stroll outside, will inevitably expose their children to the joys of the trail, perhaps nurturing a generation of environmental heroes.

Teens

A high school cross-country coach once imparted to me an interesting insight into the teenage athlete. Participation in a team sport like soccer or volleyball requires team spirit, of course, but it can also require a certain level of confidence. After all, the team depends on each individual's skill. A teen who is shy or inexperienced might not have the courage to try out for the stressful position of goalie on the hockey squad or a place on the water polo team. Some young students have never been exposed to an organized sport in elementary or middle school and don't even know where to begin. Sadly, many children also cannot afford the equipment, lessons, and training that some sports require. Most teenagers, though, can run! A school coach can attest to this on the final day of school every year, as school empties out in no time flat. It is also very clear that, given the emotional stresses experienced by today's teenagers, the wellness benefits of trail running are a gift.

Working towards running a PR is not only a confidence builder but a wonderful way to develop goal-setting skills and grit during adolescence, attributes that will certainly help prepare them for adulthood. Socialization, stress reduction, and physical fitness are obvious benefits of athletics at any age, but science is just beginning to identify the positive side effects of participation. For instance, according to the Women's Sports Foundation, girls who participate in sports during their teenage years are 20% less likely to suffer from breast cancer in adulthood (Stauroswky et al., 2009). Teens who develop a habit of road or trail running earlier in life are establishing lifestyle practices that will help keep them fit, physically healthy, and emotionally well right into adulthood.

Adults

Adults of all ages belong to the trail running community. A recent study conducted in 2022 by the Research Centre of Applied Sport, Physical Activity, and Performance surveyed participants from 28 countries (University of Central Lancashire, 2022). The study discovered that almost 65% of runners who compete in trail or ultra events are between the ages of 35 and 54. Surprisingly, fewer than 2% of the runners in this sport were between 18 and 24. Many running organizations are also cognizant of discrepancies between genders and among ethnicities. In this study, male participants made up close to 60% and females made up 40% of runners, and in North America and Europe, there is a concerning lack of ethnic diversity in the sport. Fortunately, leading organizations are making efforts to expand access to trail running for all.

Seniors Over 60, AKA Grandmasters

The experiences of trail runners in their later years of life will vary, depending on their exercise and running histories, overall health conditions, motivation levels, and even work-life-family balance. Retirees may have the advantage of having more flexible free time to train. They may have more financial resources, enabling them to travel overseas to exciting race venues. They may also be entering the "empty nest years", when caring for a young family is no longer a day-to-day commitment. Many older runners shift their focus from 10Ks or marathons to trail and ultra racing (races over 26.2 miles in distance) when they feel the desire to embrace a new life challenge. Rather than ratcheting down activity in response to age, these intrepid runners kick it up a notch. Some older runners even begin the sport once they've entered their golden years. We've all heard about the folks who celebrate an important birthday milestone by skydiving. In today's society, it is more common than ever that people believe that age is just a number and take up new physical adventures to prove it.

Of course, at every age, our incredible human physiology experiences changes and challenges. We know that as we grow older, we may experience a decline in hormone levels, reduced muscle mass, bone density issues, or even difficulties with balance and agility. Nevertheless, with strategic approaches to training, nutrition, and lifestyle, there is no reason for the Grandmaster to hit that rocking chair! With research and coaching, even the grandparents in our community can hit the trails. In fact, maintaining a physically active life will reverse or stall many of the typical limitations that can come with aging. Study after study shows that strength training helps to combat osteoporosis; increased attention to protein intake can preserve and enhance muscle mass; and healthy sleep habits can help stave off dementia and Alzheimer's. In his well-known Blue Zones work, National Geographic Explorer Dan Buettner studied pockets of longevity all over the globe and identified the lifestyle habits that account for them. In every case, physical movement, whether strenuous exercise or simply walking or gardening, is a contributor to healthier, happier, and longer lives (Buettner, 2015). Imagine, then, the health and emotional benefits for a senior trail runner.

Body Types

Just as there are no age limitations for trail running, there is also no singular ideal body type. Sure, competitive trail runners and ultra runners may develop sport-specific physical attributes, like muscular legs and slim builds, but all physiques are welcome on the trail. One trail mate of mine was hesitant to take up the sport, believing that she was, in her words, "too fat." Nevertheless, she joined a local running club. It turns out she had excellent cardiovascular fitness and impressive endurance levels. After several months of hitting the trail, she had also built considerable muscle and slimmed down a bit. More importantly, however, she had completely changed her attitude about her body. She now saw herself as strong and capable, not fat. The completion of her first race proved that she was determined, courageous, and gritty. She thanked her body for taking her on new adventures and began to adopt better nutrition, sleep, and strength training practices to enhance her running. She no longer seeks to attain a particular body type and is healthy, confident, and beautiful inside and out.

Predictably, different body types will require differentiated training and nutritional needs, particularly for runners completing frequent runs or ultras. Underweight runners may need to consume more calories during a run than those who carry more weight on their frame. Shorter people may have to pace themselves differently than those with longer strides. Those with flat feet or plantar fasciitis may have to find shoes that meet their needs more specifically. Each runner will have a unique form and can discover their ideal habits with individualized training. That's why trail running is such a beautiful sport; it is truly for everyone!

Physical and Intellectual Limitations

So, what about people with serious limitations? There is no question that trail running requires strength, stamina, and a great deal of mental and physical agility. Can those with disabilities still participate? Many heroic athletes have proven that, with the right attitude and the support of a loving team, the answer is, of course!

I often think about one of my personal heroes, Terry Fox, and the annual Terry Fox Run. The event began in Canada in 1981 and has since spread to over 19 additional countries. Terry was an 18-year-old amputee who trained to run across Canada to raise funds for cancer research. He had lost a leg just above the knee but was determined to continue his athletic career, now with an artificial limb. He inspired millions of people with his Marathon of Hope in 1980. Bravely, he ran day after day for 6 months in all kinds of weather, covering 3,339 miles before his cancer resurged, this time in his lungs, forcing him to stop. Although Terry passed away in 1981, his message to the world still rings true today: "I want to set an example that will never be forgotten" (Terry Fox Foundation, n.d.).

The Invictus Games, the Paralympic Games, and the Special Olympics are well-established events for all kinds of athletes who face limitations. They each offer a variety of sports with accommodations designed to open access to athletic competition for those with unique challenges. Trail running, naturally, requires very specific accommodations, given the difficult terrain involved.

Running for the Visually Impaired

Depending on the precise condition of a visually impaired trail runner, the challenges will vary. For some, depth perception is limited; for others, peripheral vision may be an issue; and for some, they may be completely blind. Nevertheless, with resilience, training, and support, a visually impaired runner can hit the trail. The key is to partner with a sighted running guide. Achilles International is a non-profit organization that pairs disabled athletes with sighted and able-bodied athletes. Active in 17 counties, Achilles focuses on running events for participants of all ages (Achilles International, n.d.). A running guide is trained to use voice and touch cues to communicate with the partner runner about the intricacies of the terrain. The pair train together, learn one another's running style, and learn to function as a coordinated unit. These partnerships often evolve into lifelong friendships.

Running for the Deaf Athlete

Those with hearing difficulties can benefit from technology that signals through visual or tactile cues instead. Able to navigate the trail visually, deaf runners may not need a guide but would benefit from accommodations such as flashing lights to indicate a starting buzzer or cues from race volunteers who speak sign language. Knowing the course ahead of time and identifying hazards in advance is critical preparation for all runners, but particularly important for the runner with hearing or vision loss. Of course, running with a team, club, or buddy who can communicate with sign language is ideal.

Running with Prosthetics

Amputees running with lower-body prosthetics experience a very unique challenge when it comes to trail running;

nevertheless, it's absolutely achievable. Many who run with prosthetic blades do so on flat, or at least fairly consistent, surfaces. The typical blade, however, is not designed for the complexity of the trail terrain. Blades are also pricey, and specialized versions may not always be covered by insurance. Another consideration is their maintenance; nowadays, these devices are technically complex, engineered with features that may need regular adjustment and repair. Trail running will take its toll on blades, as it does on our bodies, so planning for maintenance is as important as planning for our bodies' nutritional needs. One final challenge for amputees concerns the relationship between the prosthetic and the remaining limb segment. Sweat, improper fit, and overuse can create irritation issues, so the runner needs to plan for prevention and healing. Again, a running buddy or coach is a wonderful support, but many with prosthetics run independently. The runner may need to shift gait, slow down for rocky or muddy segments, or even slide down hills, but athletes in the sport who have gone before have shown us that anything is possible!

Pregnancy

Naturally, pregnant women should always consult with medical experts about their activity levels. In general, however, we know it is really important for a mom-to-be to remain as active as possible. The expected side effects of pregnancy, like nausea and fatigue, may slow down a pregnant runner, and the more serious conditions affecting pregnant women, like anemia and preeclampsia, may require a hiatus from rigorous exercise. Balance and coordination shift as the womb expands, so the trail runner with a bun in the oven should be especially vigilant about falls. Hydration and nutrition needs will also differ for this runner, as she is drinking and eating for two, and exposure to more extreme weather elements may affect the pregnant runner differently. Finding appropriate running gear for a growing belly and swelling feet may be a fun challenge, too.

Perhaps the most important rule, especially for a serious pregnant runner, is to be flexible with expectations and listen to her body. As she nears her due date, it is also critical that she train and race with a buddy. As beautiful as it is, the trail is not the ideal location for labor and delivery.

Injury Recovery

I recently interviewed a novice trail runner who had just turned 63. A former road runner, she had recently emerged from a six-week recovery from stress fractures in her right metatarsals, followed by a three-month hiatus as she healed from rotator cuff surgery. Her podiatrist had given her clearance to walk, initially with an orthopedic boot, but had cautioned her that her running days may be coming to a close as the fractures were repeat injuries. Her shoulder surgeon admonished her to avoid any physical activity that could jolt her shoulder. For someone who ran, practiced martial arts, and played pickle ball, the sedentary waiting period would have driven her mad. So, to save her sanity, she devoted her time to working up to 20,000 steps per day and exploring local hiking trails. On those trails, she became aware of many cheerful people buzzing past her, running the trails. It did not take long for her to get excited about a whole new challenge: trail running. Six months later, she had researched and purchased trail running shoes, crafted a training plan, and registered for her first trail race. She now runs trails 3–4 times a week, has added lap swimming to her routine to strengthen her shoulder, and has volunteered for several trail maintenance events. Most importantly, she is excited about a new passion.

In many cases, trail running may just be the ideal shift for the athlete who is recovering from a major injury. The emotional and wellness benefits gained from being outdoors are certain to aid in the healing process. In the above case, shoulder repair surgery required the athlete to stop playing pickle ball. Trail running, however, became the ideal replacement, as she could continue with cardio and prevent the stir-craziness that comes with inactivity. Foot, leg, hip, and other lower body injuries, however, may require a different approach. In some cases, slowing down to a leisurely walk or easy hike will enhance mobility and speed up the healing process. Another running mate of mine was encouraged to walk the same day he had meniscus tear repair surgery. The doctor's orders were to walk every day, steadily increasing mileage, but to stay off the treadmill. Again, the trail was the fix, and two weeks in, this individual had adopted the habit of a daily three-mile hike, a habit he continues today. In every case, the recovering athlete should consult with a medical professional to determine the ideal plan.

Runners with Intellectual Disabilities

If you ever have the chance to be a spectator at a Special Olympics event, your heart will be full when you see the joy on the faces of these very special athletes. Special Olympians compete in 5Ks, 10Ks, marathons, and Ironmans, so there is no reason a runner with an intellectual disability should not be able to train and race on the trail. As always, a coach or buddy will play an integral role in orienting the special runner to the rules of the run, how to navigate trails and read markers, and how to recognize potential hazards on the trail. Ensuring access to the sport for these individuals will enhance the wonder of this experience for us all.

Conservation Hack

The trail will grant you many gifts of health and mental wellness, so remember to respect the natural environment in return. Stay on the path and never venture into areas marked out-of-bounds. Wherever possible, take care not to break branches, disturb nests, or kick up soil. Limit noise pollution. Even our footfalls can disturb a fragile ecosystem. More importantly, pay back by joining conservation efforts like trail maintenance, tree planting, or beach clean-ups. Donate to conservation charities. Visit schools to present talks about your trail experiences. In your day-to-day life, become a trail ambassador, so we can protect access to the natural world for the next generation.

Chapter 2:

Gearing Up: Essentials for the

Trail

They say there's no such thing as bad weather, just bad gear. One of the beauties of trail running is that, unlike so many sports, the equipment expenses are minimal. However, it is still critical to invest in the gear that keeps you safe, comfortable, and injury-free. Reviews of shoes, clothing, hydration packs, and technology are readily available on the internet and in sports publications. Many equipment stores offer consulting services and even trial periods. Trail running camps and race organizers often provide participants with kit lists in advance, so as you immerse yourself in this sport, you will likely gain a good deal of knowledge about what is available. However, there is nothing more useful than conversing with other runners. As you begin to gear up, know that your running club, coach, or buddies will be excellent sources of advice. Those who run on the same trails as you will have tried and true experience in similar running environments, and those who have experience further afield will be able to advise you on how to gear up for your next adventure.

Choosing the Right Shoes

The human foot is a miracle of engineering. Comprised of hundreds of bones, joints, muscles, ligaments, tendons, and nerves, our feet are designed to bear our body weight and mobilize us for a lifetime. Healthy stability, posture, and balance for the entire body depend on healthy feet. Our feet work very hard for us, so we need to take good care of them! Not surprisingly, the most important element of a trail runner's gear is the shoe. Just think of how many steps a runner takes during a run, not to mention the incredible versatility of the mechanism that carries us up and down slopes, through muddy swamps, and over sandy, rocky, or compact terrain. If there is a piece of running equipment worth investing in, it is good trail shoes.

Finding the right shoe is probably one of the hardest things for a runner because everyone's feet are so different. For years, I just ran in brands that friends used or picked shoes based on their catchy colors or designs. Somehow, this worked miraculously for several years, until one pair of shoes caused a stress fracture in my knee. This occurred while I was training for a marathon due to the design's lack of compatibility with my foot. That particular shoe works great for many people but just wasn't right for me, which unfortunately led to some major setbacks and time off to heal. Then, several years later, I started to develop plantar fasciitis due to the shoes I was training in. The pain became so intense that I was almost to the point of giving up running completely. I remember going into a local running store totally defeated and in pain. I asked for their help, and they gave me a newer brand of shoe to try on. I was very hesitant, but I was also desperate, so I bought the shoes and gave them a try. Within one week, my plantar fasciitis was completely gone. While this result is probably not common, it was clear to me that I had found the shoe that worked for me, and I have not had any issues since then.

Understanding Trail Shoes

Sneakers, tennis shoes, cross-trainers, cleats, hiking boots, gym shoes, court shoes...how on earth is a person to sort out all the varieties of footwear available to athletes? Perhaps the most important thing to know is that trail shoes are designed differently than running or hiking shoes in general. It is certainly worthwhile to read reviews of various shoes prior to purchasing a pair, as there are many variations in both design and pricing.

Trail shoes are designed with uneven surfaces and varied terrain in mind. On any given run, you may encounter rocks, sand, mud, grass, turf, exposed tree roots, or all of the above. The ideal shoe, then, must be able to handle all kinds of surfaces. Unlike the average road shoe, which is generally geared towards flat surfaces, the trail shoe must address stability, shock absorption, and flexibility. Trail shoes are heavier and tougher than road shoes, but lighter and more flexible than hiking shoes. Although trail shoes share the same features as road shoes in general, the quality of those features can differ.

Soles

The material that lines the bottom of the shoe from heel to toe is called the outsole. In trail shoes, these are made of tougher material in order to cope with rocks, roots, and other natural elements that could tear through lighter material. On the bottom side of the outsole are teeth, or "lugs". These work to grip the surface and add traction and protection. Depending on the terrain, trail shoes can come with a variety of lug designs.

Rock Plate

The rock plate is located along the top of the outsole. Made of carbon or rigid plastic, the purpose of the rock plate is to prevent sharp objects from piercing through the midsole of your shoe. The rock plate may make the shoe feel less flexible than a road shoe, which can take some getting used to for those transitioning to the trail.

Midsole

The midsole lies along the rock plate. Its purpose is to provide cushioning, which can range in texture from soft to rigid. This is where a runner may wish to try out various shoes to determine the ideal personal comfort level.

Heel

The heel of the trail shoe has several elements. The heel cup is the concave segment that cradles the heel. To add stability to the heel, some trail shoes have a heel counter, which is essentially a rigid piece of material that holds the heel in place.

Toe Box and Toe Cap

The toe box is the wider end of the shoe and can be rounded or tapered, depending on the shape of the runner's toes. On the outside, the toe box is typically protected by a toe cap, which is made of stronger material. Its purpose is to protect the toe from trail hazards. One of the distinctive features of the trail shoe is a larger, thicker toe cap than what is usually found on a road shoe.

Overlay

The overlay is the material on top of the upper material of the shoe. In trail shoes, the overlay is heavier and stronger than it is in road shoes, again to protect the shoe and the foot from trail hazards. The thicker, stronger material used for the overlay causes the trail shoe to have less ventilation than the road shoe. The benefit of this may be that the shoe is also more water resistant.

Tongue

Another distinction between a trail shoe and a road shoe is that in the former, the tongue is sometimes stitched to the sides of the upper or overlay in order to minimize the amount of trail debris that might make its way into the shoe.

Fit

We've all heard the adage, "If the shoe fits, wear it." So, what do you look for in the perfect fit? While a shoe may seem comfortable in the shop when you try it on and walk a few steps, will it still be comfortable when you've run 50 miles in it? With experience on the trail, of course, every runner will develop an appreciation for which features work best. However, keep in mind that foot shape can change over time, race conditions vary, and injuries may require different kinds of support. In general, the ideal trail shoe must provide a balance of stability and flexibility.

The toe box should allow for ample movement for your toes and sides of your feet while also providing stability for your foot and ankle. Toe boxes that are too small prevent toes from splaying naturally and can cause toes to pound against the end of the shoes. Painful blisters, calluses, and corns can result from cramped toes, and the blackening or loss of toenails can result from repeated pounding. On the other hand (or foot), toe boxes that are too roomy can decrease the foot's stability, which can also result in stress on and injury to the ankle.

Similarly, the overlay of the shoe must balance both ample space and good stability for the foot. For example, runners with high arches might need a more generous overlay than those with more petite feet. Keep in mind that over time and with many miles accrued, your foot shape is likely to evolve, so a shoe that feels comfortable one season may not work as well the next year.

The heel cup and counter should fit closely enough to keep your heel stable and prevent your foot from rubbing up and down against the shoe, which will cause painful blisters. A heel that is too tight will potentially cause the same blister issue and restrict your foot's natural movements.

Some runners, particularly those with plantar fasciitis, shin splints, or pre-existing foot, knee, hip, or back pain, may choose to insert arch supports or orthotics into their shoes. These devices help to improve posture, thereby reducing stress on the joints. In these cases, the wearer will likely need to increase the shoe size.

When shopping for trail shoes, you may come across the term "zero drop". Drop refers to the difference in height from the heel to the toe of the shoe. Trail shoes tend to have a zero drop or lower drop (i.e., less difference between the height of the heel and toe), as this tends to shift the foot from a heel strike to a more neutral strike. It can take some time to become accustomed to a zero drop shoe where the toe and heel are level, but runners often remark that this works better on uphill and downhill slopes and uneven surfaces and increases the sense of connection with the ground.

Whatever the case, with the complex mechanics involved in the trail shoe, it's always advisable to do your research and work with a coach or salesperson who understands the sport of trail running and the importance of determining the ideal personalized fit.

Functionality

Long-Term Comfort

The most important element of your chosen shoe is, of course, comfort. As you take on longer and longer runs, your definition of comfort might shift, as your shoes will need to carry you over many miles and through rough terrain. It is not uncommon to change shoes every 300–500 miles, depending on wear and tear, so you should be aware of the mileage you are accruing and expect to purchase new shoes once or twice a year.

Water Resistance

Because trail terrain will inevitably take you through rain, snow, mud, and ponds, water resistance is also an important feature. Imagine slogging through a 10K run with dripping wet feet! Limiting your feet's exposure to moisture is a must.

Durability

Durability is obviously another consideration. Your shoes will be assaulted by rocks, tree roots, sand, scratchy plants, and many of nature's other obstacles. To do their job of protecting your feet, your shoes need to be constructed of tough materials.

Color

If you choose your trail shoes based only on their attractive color scheme, you are in for a disappointment! Your shoes will be filthy as soon as you hit the trail, so fashion should not be a priority. Having brightly colored or reflective strips on your shoes, however, is a great idea, especially if you are planning on running at night. Anything you can do to increase your safety is a win.

Conservation Hack

In an effort to support the green, circular economy, some footwear companies offer recycling services. Drop-off boxes, donation centers, resale programs, and return-by-mail services are some of the ways you can ensure that your shoes do not end up in landfills.

Essential Gear

Choosing your running gear need not be a wardrobe challenge. Your greatest investment will be your shoes, but you will have lots of fun selecting a collection of running attire. With so many athletic brands available, you'll have a range of choices that do not break the bank.

Clothing

Comfort, safety, and versatility should be your prime considerations when selecting your running clothing. Your choices will be determined in large part by your local climate and weather patterns, whether you will run at night or in daylight, and the terrain of the trails you plan to conquer. You will soon discover that layers are the solution, particularly if you take on longer runs. In warm weather, your gear list will include tanks, tee shirts, long-sleeved shirts, shorts, leggings, socks, and a cap. You will want to be aware of the dangers of sun exposure and cover up as much as possible. In windy, cold, or wet weather, you'll want to add a base layer, tights, gaiters, pullovers, shells, fleece, a rain jacket, gloves, and a warm hat. You need to be careful to avoid hypothermia and frostbite! Dress in bright colors or add reflective tape so that you are highly visible on your runs, especially at night.

Regardless of the temperature, you will want to choose clothing that is lightweight, breathable, water-resistant, and UV-protective. On a long run, chances are you will carry some of your gear until you need it, so choose gear that is easy to put on and take off. Zippers are a favorite here, and pullovers work well too.

Experience will soon teach you that sweating and chafing are your enemies on the trail, so experiment with your choices to see which breathes most effectively for you. Contemporary athletic wear designers utilize some of the most high-tech fabrics we know of. Many of these fabrics are constructed from synthetic materials specifically formulated to prevent or resolve exposure to moisture, UV rays, and even insects. One easy mantra to remember is that "cotton is rotten." Although cotton is a lovely, natural material, it acts as a moisture wick. Once wet, it retains moisture, which is a serious pitfall for the runner who needs to maintain a consistent body temperature. For chafing, some runners prefer to go commando and just wear compression shorts, leaving those uncomfortable undies behind. Others quickly learn the value of anti-chafing cream!

Conservation Hack

Many athletic apparel companies are at the forefront of conservation efforts, setting a wonderful example for consumers. As you research clothing, you may want to support their efforts by purchasing items made from recycled fabrics or bamboo and shopping with companies that prioritize sustainable and ethical practices. Some companies even sell used gear, so you may find a treasure or two if you look around. Just remember to avoid cotton!

Hydration Systems

Regardless of the terrain, weather, and length of your run, you never want to be without water and/or electrolytes. Dehydration, sunburn, heat exhaustion, and heat stroke are all hazards that can be easily avoided. Hydration carriers come in all sorts of styles, ranging from simple soft flasks to more complex hydration vests or backpacks. You will want to think about the volume of water you need, easy access to the water, and balanced placement. Carrying a water bottle in one hand is not only awkward but can also throw off a runner's posture. So even on a short run, carry a waist pack or vest to hold your water bottle. Running hands-free allows a runner to efficiently deal with obstacles, climb, and even break a fall. Choose a hydration system that is lightweight, not too bulky, easy to access, and hands-free.

For those running long races deep into the wilderness, an additional safeguard is a water filtration device like a LifeStraw. These devices come in very simple styles, so they are not difficult to carry. A runner lost on the trail will never regret taking this friend along.

Accessories

Create a checklist for yourself and think about whether you need any of these additional accessories whenever you plan a run or race: sunscreen, lip balm, sunglasses, eyeglasses, whistle, first aid supplies, compass, topographical map, camera, cellphone, knife, insect repellant, pepper spray, and noisemakers. For a short run, you won't need much, and for a lengthy run, you'll not want to carry pounds of gear, so be strategic, but make sure you have what you need. Ultra runs might involve shelters, space blankets, and medical supplies. This is where a club or coach is extremely useful. Experienced runners will have good advice for novices about what to pack for each situation.

Tech Talk

Having the right technology can certainly enhance the trail runner's experience, too. There is no need to spend a fortune, though, on the latest gadgets. Many useful tools are located right on your smartphone: SOS features, flashlight, compass, mapping applications, emergency alert systems, and location-sharing applications. Just remember to power up your phone fully before heading out, and find a waist pack that fits just right so you can carry the phone comfortably. If you're going on a longer run or overnight travel, consider carrying a spare battery charger or solar charger.

Tracking and Safety

In addition to the handy smartphone, many tracking tools are at your disposal. High-tech fitness watches can monitor location, distance, elevation, speed, step counts, mileage, and heart rate. Many runners already own such watches, so gaining these tools may not incur additional expense. Dedicated GPS units can be really useful, particularly in the wild, as they tend to be more accurate than fitness watches. These devices, however, can cost upwards of several hundred dollars. It is well worth the time to experiment with GPS devices and practice while you are training on shorter, easier runs. You do not want to be figuring out which application to open or how to use your tools when you are in an urgent situation.

For evening or night runs, or even for runs in inclement weather, lighting is also something to consider. Headlamps are easy to wear, and in addition to aiding your vision, they help others see you. A small flashlight is also useful, particularly in a difficult section of trail or when a signaling device is needed. Again, be sure your electronics are powered up and consider a spare battery when relevant.

Communication

In spite of the allure of peace and quiet on the trail, maintaining communication with others is critical for your safety. Hopefully, your smartphone is an easy connection to civilization; however, it is not unusual to encounter poor connectivity on the trail. In those cases, satellite messengers can transmit your location, messages, and, if necessary, SOS signals. Walkie-talkie radio devices are useful among participants on the same trails but may have limited range. Even the humble flashlight can be used to communicate. The most important tool, though, is common sense. Before every run or race, report your departure time, route, and anticipated finish time to a responsible buddy who will send out help if you do not return home when expected.

A Word About Ear Buds

Many runners enjoy listening to music or an inspirational audiobook while training. There is no doubt that the distraction and focus provided by your auxiliary audio can ease your run and counter boredom (not that you will ever become bored on the trail!) On the contrary, trail running requires you to be 100% focused on your immediate environment. Think about it: with earbuds in and music blaring, can you be alert to any nearby hazards? Can you communicate effectively with other runners if you cannot hear what is happening around you? The same goes for road runners. Alertness to traffic and other urban or suburban noise is essential to a runner's safety. Although you might be in the habit of listening to music or podcasts, you will miss out on so much beauty if you drown out the natural music of the trail. If you absolutely must wear ear buds while you run, stay safer by keeping only one in so you can still hear the ambient noise of the outdoors, or invest in bone-conducting headphones to keep your ears free. You may want to consider investing in water-resistant or waterproof headphones to counter any sweat or inclement weather you incur on the trail.

Chapter 3:

From Pavement to Path:

Transitioning to Trail Running

The Art of Adaptation

I was a runner for over 7 years before even setting foot on a trail, but once I gave it a try, I was hooked. On my very first trail run, I laced up my clean new trail shoes, excited about a new route for the morning. Because I knew that trail terrain would be new for me, I decided to warm up easily by running down the street to a local park instead of driving down and parking. This way, I could start on a solid, level road and then eventually move on to the sandy, grassy, rocky, and hilly trails found in the park. As I expected, I made a number of discoveries. Running downhill in loose grit is scary. If there are dog walkers in your park, watch out for poop. The drinking fountain doesn't always work. On a slanted section of trail, your left and right feet hit the ground at different angles, which is tricky for your ankles. Shifting from sand to grass is not a smooth transition. Pine needles are slippery! The automatic irrigation system kicks in when you least expect it. Most importantly, I understood right away that road running is way less complicated than the trail, but the trail is much more interesting and fun.

When I got home from that early run, I had clocked a mile more than my usual route. My left ankle was complaining, I had gained a few new blisters, and my new shoes, well, they were filthy. In other words, I had enjoyed a great run!

Every trail runner is going to be a little battered and bruised. Muscle soreness, minor injuries, and lots of blisters are simply part of the game. New equipment requires patience and adjustment. The terrain itself necessitates constant adaptation. The same trail you conquered in the spring can present a whole new range of challenges in the winter.

It's important to remember that the need to constantly adapt on the trail is what makes this sport so exciting. Say good-bye to the rhythmic pounding of feet in an urban marathon and say hello to adventure!

Building Trail-Worthy Fitness

Transitioning from running roads to trails is harder than you would anticipate if you are used to the fast pace of the marathon world. There are many different techniques that become ingrained in you when road running, such as: when in a race, you aim to run the whole time. In trail running, you learn that you expend unnecessary energy running up steeper hills and likely do not get up the hill any faster than you would power hiking. Even if you run up the hill, you will most likely have to catch your breath at the top due to the energy you expended. In the end, it takes more time to recover from the exertion than it takes to power hike up a hill. Another major transition for road runners is simply the technicality of the trail. While you do get to enjoy nature and see some amazing sights while running in the woods, you must always be aware of your surroundings and pay attention to each step. On a road, if you get tired and start shuffling your feet a little due to fatigue, you will most likely be okay and able to continue. If you start to shuffle your feet on a trail, you will most likely end up hitting a root, rock, empty air, or something that will cause you to fall, so it is important to always be focused on what's ahead of you and to pick up your feet.

Overall, trail running fitness entails more than building physical strength and cardiovascular endurance. It requires coordination, balance, mental agility, and emotional resilience. Imagine the long-term health benefits of a sport that puts this all together in one package!

Physical Strength

General strength training is an essential part of trail running fitness. Although we tend to be cognizant of joint issues, your whole body will need to be strong and healthy. A balanced approach to strength training with your lower body, core, and upper body will keep you in the best form. While it is easy to see the benefit of targeting large muscle groups like your quads or glutes, it is equally important to attend to those little muscles that help with agility and flexibility.

Your toes and feet are going to take a beating, so try doing toe curls while you watch TV or walk barefoot at the beach. Your ankles will definitely work hard for you, so add some ankle pushups while you wash dishes! We run with our arms, which move in opposition to our legs, so pick up a dumbbell and do some curls while you wait for coffee to brew. Even adopting simple strength movements with regularity will build trail-running muscles.

For a serious runner, however, the best approach is to connect with a professional strength trainer who can match your strength goals to your running goals. Many gyms offer free training, and many running clubs offer this kind of service with minimal cost. There are also plenty of online fitness programs, apps, and services that can support your strength training goals.

As with so many endeavors, athletes can get injured when they overdo it. Remember to ease into any training regimen and consult with experts so you avoid injury. Make sure you practice correct form as you train, and celebrate the incremental successes you experience. If you pull a muscle, don't push through the pain. Stop and rest, and give yourself time to heal. A runner's most frustrating issue is having to take a hiatus from training to heal an injury. You never want to miss a race because you were training too hard!

Cardiovascular Fitness

Cardiovascular fitness is the capacity of the heart and lungs to transport oxygenated blood to the many components of the body This type of fitness is built up over time. Many studies have concluded that increasing cardio training results in decreased illness, particularly heart disease, and potentially even dementia. One measure of cardiovascular fitness is VO2max testing, which some competitive athletes undergo in a laboratory setting. Most runners, though, estimate their cardiovascular fitness by measuring heart rate and pulse data while exercising or by simply observing their improving endurance levels over time.

Common exercises that get your heart beating are, of course, running, swimming, jumping rope, cycling, and rowing. All of these will support a runner's training. Runners who are on a break due to a lower body injury might be interested in aqua-jogging. With access to the deep end of a pool, even someone healing a fractured foot can mimic the motions of running while in the water and still get a fabulous workout.

It is easier to measure gains in cardiovascular fitness on road runs, a treadmill, or an elliptical machine than by judging improved performance on the trail. This is because the many variables in trail running entail various speeds and degrees of physical effort. This can actually be beneficial to your fitness as your heart and respiratory system learn to accelerate and downshift efficiently. For a novice trail runner, however, there is no need to get too technical about data. You will feel the improvement as you train. Many athletes use an informal metric called Rate of Perceived Exertion, or RPE. Using this scale conceived by Gunnar Borg, the athlete notes the level of exertion experienced during the workout, scores the exertion level from one to ten (ten being very rigorous), and collects data over time regarding any changes.

Runners are well-known for their persistence, so it is critical to understand that risks may lie in overdoing it with cardio. Dizziness, unusual shortness of breath, chest pain, and nausea can all be signs of excessive stress on the heart or lungs, so if something feels wrong, stop and get medical attention.

Physical Agility and Balance

Agility and balance are even more important in trail running than in traditional road running. Because the terrain constantly presents new features, the body constantly adjusts. Swerves in the path, shifts in ascent or descent, uneven surfaces, and a route that acts like an obstacle course demand that the runner develop superior agility. Runners used to training on a treadmill, which provides a consistent pace and surface, will need to develop the muscles, joints, and tendons that allow for sudden and frequent changes in speed, direction, and foot strike. Imagine transitioning from clambering up a steep, rocky rise to running down a series of zigzagging switchbacks on unstable gravel. This is no easy feat, and it is not easy on the feet!

Building up the small muscles that assist with mobility and flexibility is a must, and your strength training will certainly support this. Enhancing the strength of your joints, particularly your ankles, knees, and hips, is equally important and will happen naturally as you accumulate more miles. Adding a daily stretching and balance regimen will complement the strength and cardio training that you have already integrated into your fitness plan. This might include yoga, pilates, using resistance bands, or practicing Tai Chi. Simple habits you can adopt at home will also help. Stand on one foot while brushing your teeth. Practice moving from sitting on the floor to standing up without using your arms. While watching television, rather than sitting on the couch, plop yourself on that yoga mat or balance ball and stretch those muscles!

Developing strong balance is also critical. You may find yourself nearing a narrow trail segment overlooking a cliff or drop-off. At other times, you may need to navigate across a swamp on a narrow, makeshift bridge or through a maze of sharp boulders. Good balance will add efficiency to your running style and keep you safe. Just remember, though, that even with excellent agility and balance, you will take a fall now and then. However, you will likely be able to pick yourself up again with no problem.

Endurance

Imagine that you have already completed 5K and 10K trail runs or that you are a former marathoner. Now, you want to take on the challenge of a 50-mile ultra race. An ultra is a race longer than a marathon (26.2 miles). You are mentally ready and excited about a new adventure. In fact, you feel like you could do it tomorrow!

Wait. Now you will need to build stamina and train for endurance, not speed. Understand that you are not going to shift immediately from a fast 5K pace to an endurance run that might take 8 hours to complete. Every runner's body will need plenty of time training in order to develop this kind of endurance, and that training will encompass cardiovascular, strength, agility, and balance work. In a sense, your body is undergoing a total reset as it develops muscle, circulation capacity, and tendon flexibility, so devise a long-term plan. You will need patience.

You will also need to understand the distinction between feeling tired and being fatigued. When we've expended a great deal of energy in any physical pursuit, we are bound to feel tired, particularly after we've cooled down a bit. Most runners feel a relaxed kind of tired after a rigorous run. Fatigue, though, is concerning. If a runner experiences nausea, headaches, dizziness, loss of appetite, moodiness, or low motivation, a serious level of exhaustion may be the issue. In this case, powering through is a bad idea. Pushing past the point of fatigue will not help build your endurance and might set you up for a long recovery period.

Set short-term goals and measure your endurance by recording small wins over time. Don't be afraid of setbacks, as they will definitely happen; this will be a "two steps forward, one step back" endeavor. Recruit a team of cheerleaders who can urge you on and celebrate your milestones.

Training Plans and Their Components

Perhaps the most important thing to know about training plans is that they never go according to plan! It may sound contradictory, but plan to ditch the plan from time to time when life gets complicated. Anticipate that you will experience interruptions and disappointments, and know that it is the overall plan that counts, not whether you reach each goal every week. The old adage "go slow to go fast" is a great reminder that patience takes effort to develop, and long-term gains are the target.

Training plans will no doubt vary depending on the age, fitness level, and goals of the individual runner. The time and schedule available to the runner will also need to be considered when crafting a plan. There are many apps and services available to help with the process, but it is paramount to remember the unique needs of each athlete. A novice runner might begin with a plan to simply increase time on the pavement. Then, hiking or speed-walking on trails might be added. Eventually, as a runner becomes stronger and builds endurance, this sport will become more time-consuming, so today's plan might look very different from that of six months ago or six months from now. In general, a solid training plan should include a schedule of runs that vary in length and difficulty, strength training sessions, and a menu of stretching and flexibility exercises to be practiced on a regular basis.

High-Intensity Interval Training (HIIT)

As a runner's cardiovascular endurance becomes stronger, adding High-Intensity Interval Training, or HIIT, will help push their stamina even further. The HIIT entails increasing the intensity of exercise for a short duration and then following with a period of lower intensity. This is a great way for a new runner to attack hills. If you can't make it the whole way up a hill, run all out for 15 seconds and then follow with a walk or slow jog for one minute. Then repeat. Before long, the ratio will shift to 20 seconds/55 seconds, then to 25 seconds/50 seconds. You will also notice that, in general, your recovery times, even for non-HIIT runs, will decrease in duration. Many studies have been conducted on the health benefits of HIITs, which include weight loss, improved oxygen consumption, reduced blood pressure, and overall improved cardiovascular performance (Kluwer, 2021). HIITs can easily be done at home too, and they don't take much time. Jumping rope, burpees, jumping jacks, and the dreaded high knees are all excellent HIIT activities.

Tempo Runs

Tempo runs are another strategy that many trail runners use. These involve running at a pace slightly higher than your typical long-distance pace, but for a shorter length of time. Because you are pushing a little harder during a tempo run, it is really important to listen to your body and keep your run to a sustainable duration. Initially, the tempo pace will be uncomfortable but doable; ultimately, over time, what used to be your tempo pace will now seem very comfortable: time to set another, quicker pace.

Fartlek Runs

Believe it or not, fartlek runs are not runs where you pass gas. The word comes from Swedish and means "speed play". A fartlek run is an unstructured run where you experiment with different speeds and directions for different durations; basically, it is running around all over the place! When you think about it, this is a great way to approximate the constantly changing dynamics of the trail. Of course, on a road run, a racer experiences a range of cadence, but not nearly to the same degree as a trail runner. So, practicing runs where the pace, direction, and elevation are frequently changing teaches your body to adapt to the trail. Think about when you were a child playing tag. You were obviously running. Were your runs structured? Did they have a consistent pace? Did you run behind trees and over hills and fences? Did you stop and go, speed up, and slow down? Did you have fun? You didn't realize it, but you were doing a fartlek! And I bet when you were a child, you would have loved to have known that word!

Developing Your Form

A runner's form, like any athlete's, is incredibly important. A new runner will need time and experience to figure out what works best. Your form is made up of elements like posture; stride; heel, toe, or neutral strike; the coordination of arms and legs; length of gait; and the degree to which you use your core efficiently. Clearly, while running or speed-walking up a steep hill, your form will look and feel a lot different from the form needed to trudge through knee-high wet grass.

One way to develop good form is to work with a coach who can observe your natural movement patterns to help you break poor habits and form good ones. You might see this service referred to as gait analysis. Again, however, not everyone wants to hire a coach, especially those new to the sport. Those who run with buddies can always ask their buddies to comment on what they see. Any friend can be asked to video-tape you, so you can see for yourself. A friend of mine burst into laughter after viewing a video I took of her. "I had no idea I ran with my elbows sticking out! I look like a chicken!" she chuckled. Then it was my turn to laugh. "But did you notice that you also stick out your tongue?"

A clever trick I learned to check on your form is to look closely at your shadow when you are running behind it. Are your shoulders level? Do your hips seem to be balanced? Are you slumping or leaning back too far? What can you tell from the shape and movement of your shadow? You may even be able to identify asymmetries that could lead to injury over time or overuse issues like pounding harder than necessary. Something else to think about is whether you are wasting movement. During an ultra run, every unnecessary movement expends the energy that a runner may need to rely on later. Finally, remember that your form will evolve as your strength, endurance, and flexibility improve, so be aware, but don't stress over small issues.

The Importance of Rest and Recovery

Good sleep hygiene is essential for all human beings, athletic or not. A lack of deep sleep can result in stress, high blood pressure, illness, a lowered immune response, and overall grouchiness. Cognitive issues like confusion, slow mental processing, and forgetfulness can also be due to a lack of sleep. On the bright side, runners who have just completed a strenuous run will report that they often benefit from deeper, longer sleeps than when they are not running. Some comment that they frequently take a short nap after a long run. Sleep is fundamental to your body's healing processes, so when you are planning a running and workout schedule, be sure to prioritize bedtime and plan ahead. If you have a short, fast run planned for 6:00 am tomorrow morning, tonight is not the best time to stay out late. On the other hand, if you have an important social engagement that will keep you up late, move your early morning run to another day. Inform yourself about barriers to a good night's sleep, like excessive screen time, late afternoon caffeine, alcohol consumption, working late, or just plain worrying. Instead, learn about practices that enhance your sleep habits. Perhaps a video yoga class works for you. Maybe meditation before bed helps you to slow down. Herbal tea, a 15-minute stretch, an evening walk, or calming music might be the fix. I once had a friend who kept her college economics textbook by her bedside. It was so boring, picking it up worked every time! Whatever you do, remember that plenty of sleep will grant you plenty of energy.

Entire rest days are also really important. These can sometimes seem frustrating to runners who are intent on accomplishment—it's hard to stay still when you are a runner! Know that rest days are not necessarily sedentary days. Think about how you can include active rest days into your routine. Going for a slow, relaxed hike with a non-running friend is still great exercise. A refreshing swim followed by a sauna or hot tub soak will do wonders for relaxation. Table tennis, pickleball, or dance classes will use different muscles than your running mechanics demand, so you will still be resting. Plain old dog-waking will keep those muscles limber, and your canine friend will thank you too! The number of rest days you need will depend not only on your training schedule but also on your age and fitness level, whether your work life is physically strenuous, or if you are lugging small children around all day. Just remember to include rest days when you create a weekly running plan and adjust as necessary.

Typically, good sleep habits and well-planned rest days will keep you healthy and in vigorous condition. Time on the trail, however, is hard on your body, no matter how well you take care of your health. If you experience a minor injury, you'll have to modify your training plan to allow for some healing. You can't run today if you overdid it yesterday and returned home with screaming blisters. A twisted ankle is not going to improve if you run on it. Even a sunburn can be an issue if you are not protecting your skin from additional chafing and sweating. Be kind to yourself and wait it out until you are able to run comfortably.

Many athletes include foam rollers in their post-workout routines in order to speed up recovery. Icing is also a must, particularly when breaking in the joints and muscles that may not be used to the new rigors of trail running. Many topical ointments are available over the counter to ease minor aches, but for more serious pain, more support may be needed. One such cause for concern is Delayed-Onset Muscle Soreness, commonly referred to by runners as DOMS. DOMS is not unusual, particularly for long-distance runners. It usually sets in a day or two after the finish of an event. It can be really painful, though. Hydrating, rest, massage, and taking over-the-counter pain medication are among the recovery strategies used by runners who experience this kind of setback. Of course, any individual seeking relief from serious pain should consult a medical professional.

Major injuries are another situation. Fractured or broken bones, serious illness, or recent surgeries are going to require a hiatus and are always a huge disappointment. It can be really difficult for a runner to stop for a prolonged period of time. This is particularly true for beginners. If you have just jumped into the sport, gathered your gear together, joined a club, and established a plan, nothing could be more frustrating than having to stop, literally, in your tracks. This is when that emotional resilience comes in. You will have to engage in self-talk that reminds you that this is painful and disappointing, but it is temporary. Finding other activities to pursue while you heal will be really important, so take this time to read up on the sport, watch training videos, or cheerlead at actual races. You can still enjoy the sport from the sidelines.

The best advice for new runners is to listen to your body and remember the importance of flexibility. Plan to train and rest so that you do not have to miss your workouts, but when you need to change it up, be resilient and patient and consider your overall, long-term health first.

Trail Etiquette

Just as in every aspect of life, interacting with those around us can be a positive or stressful experience. Awareness of others, courtesy, and good communication are tools that ensure life runs smoothly, not to mention safely. The world of running is no exception.

On Your Left!

Etiquette on the trail is also something new for runners to learn. It is a known practice when passing another runner or hiker to yell "on the left" and pass the person on the left side. This is especially important on a narrow trail. It is also something most people on the trail are used to, and they will instinctively move to the right to allow you room. This is frequently necessary on a multi-use trail where cyclists will either ring a bell to alert you or say "on your left" or "bike back," which is a notice for you to move to the right and allow them to pass. It is also important to notify other runners behind you of a biker or runner coming in the opposite direction by yelling "runner/biker up." This way, everyone can begin moving over and letting that person pass so that no one gets injured or surprised by the encounter. Different from roads, trails can become very narrow and are often "single track," which means that they are only wide enough for one person at a time, so communication during your run is important for your safety as well as the safety of others.

Uphill / Downhill Right of Way

Running uphill is much more strenuous than running downhill. Running downhill can also be tricky, as your feet often want to go faster than you are ready for. Runners passing one another in opposite directions typically assume the right of way goes to the uphill runner, but if you encounter a downhiller flying past you with a panicked facial expression, it might just be wise to move aside.

Common Sense and Respect

Obviously, the most important thing is to use common sense to keep yourself and other runners safe. Be constantly aware of the surroundings and the presence of other runners. Follow signage about hazards, trail markers, and local rules and regulations. Avoid using headphones or ear buds, as they will limit your awareness and your ability to communicate. Even if there is no one currently passing on your left, keep the trail clear by moving to the right to stretch, hydrate, or rest. Don't make sudden turns, particularly when running in a pack. Communicate with hand signals or your voice if you need to slow down, so those behind you can pivot. No one needs to end a race prematurely because of a crash! Always remember that a smile, a thank you, a please, or a thumbs up goes a long way in terms of building community with those who share the trail.

It may seem obvious that a runner needs to respect the environment as well as the other runners, but we are sometimes surprised by human behavior. Don't relieve yourself, spit, or blow your nose on the trail unless you absolutely have to. Wait for the rest stop or first aid station. In an ultra, though, it is very common to have to relieve yourself along the way, and it is also recognized as acceptable. However, good etiquette is to remove yourself far enough off the trail to not be in others' way. For urination, it's easy to simply find a spot off the trail to respectfully cover yourself. Don't expose anyone else to an unwanted show. Defecation can be a bit trickier, as it is proper etiquette to find a more secluded spot, not too far off the trail but far away enough to be respectful of others. Following the rules of Leave No Trace, try to make sure you're well away from water sources and camps (200 feet is recommended). Find a stick to dig a hole, ideally 6–8 inches deep, to relieve yourself. After you have done your business, cover it back up as much as possible, even if it's just with rock, brush, dirt, or whatever is nearby. Many trail runners joke that pooping in the woods is the official stamp of a tried-and-true trail runner. It's going to happen, and it's okay. Remember "everybody poops ". Get it done, be respectful, and laugh it off. These tales make for good post-race stories.

Race day itself calls for additional etiquette tips. No doubt competitors are excited, distracted, and nervous, so it's even more important to be spatially aware. Don't jostle or shove others at the start line. If you are a slower runner, start at the back of the pack. You'll find your perfect lane as the crowd thins. Be cheerful and polite to race volunteers. They offer water, nutrition, and encouragement. If you see another runner in trouble, stop to offer assistance. Unlike a road race, you have a long way to go in an ultra, and taking that extra minute to help a fallen runner, thank an aid station helper, or slow down to chat with a runner that is mentally struggling won't sabotage your goals. If anything, it will set you more on fire and be a way to show others that they can do the same. There's nothing as wonderful as another runner drowning out the sound of your screaming blisters with an encouraging "Whoo hoo! You've got this!" Above all, never cut corners. Never, ever cheat! Maintain your integrity; it is far more important than your finishing time. There is absolutely no glory in a race dishonestly run, and a clean race is always a win, regardless of how long it takes to cross the finish line.

Surprise Lessons From the Road to Trail Transition

When first making the shift between running on the road and running on the trail, I learned that I could even adapt my road runs to accommodate my new sport. I didn't necessarily have to choose one or the other. Rather than running on a flat track or treadmill, I began to challenge myself in new ways during road runs. Instead of focusing solely on distance and time, I looked for opportunities to sprint up staircases, run up hills, and jog on surfaces like mud and sand. Each of these honed a different skill that I could then transfer to the trail. There was even a time when my child was very small and I could not always get away for long runs. I soon learned that running circles in the backyard while they were sleeping was a great way to adjust to uneven ground. Trail running has taught me about flexibility and how to pivot when necessary. These are skills I've really begun to appreciate—skills that have become essential to my life on and off the trail.

Chapter 4:

Conquering the Elements: Trail Terrain and Conditions

Trails consist of many elements. These include old logging roads, converted rail beds, fire roads, dried river beds, goat paths, and groomed pathways, among others. There is no single definition of a trail. Due to the constantly shifting terrain, trail runners typically run at a slower pace compared to road runners. Therefore, it is important not to become discouraged when transitioning to this type of running. With time and experience, every trail runner will increase their speed. However, in the early stages, many learn to judge a run based on exertion and time on the trail rather than speed. In fact, there is a real beauty in this. The trail runner cannot afford to obsess over finishing time since there are too many variables that can influence it. For many, simply finishing the trail is a victory in itself!

This was one of my biggest struggles in the beginning. I began in the faction of running where talent and the right to call yourself a runner were based on pace and speed. There was a time when I trained to get faster and hoped to qualify for the Boston Marathon so I could be a "real runner." While this is perfect for many runners, and they love the competitiveness and speed of the challenge, I found it discouraging. It made me feel insecure about my running abilities. So, as you can imagine, when I switched over to trail running and was even slower, I was mortified. I wouldn't even post my runs on Strava, a social media application geared towards sharing workouts with others and also a great tool for a beginner who does not yet have a watch to track mileage. I was embarrassed at how slow I was. I knew that I had climbed hills and navigated rocky terrain, but in my head, I still should have done it faster. This was a very difficult mindset for me to break, and it took a lot of time and talking with other trail runners to finally be okay with owning my pace. Over time, I have learned to love my running and be proud of what my body can do regardless of pace, but it is definitely an adjustment.

Types of Trails

Loop

A loop trail starts and ends at the same location. On a loop trail, runners will all run in the same direction.

Out-and-Back

An out-and-back trail also begins and ends at one location. A turn-around point at the halfway mark sends runners back to the start, the way they came. On this kind of trail, a runner will pass others going in the opposite direction, so the trail might be wider at certain points. If it isn't, the runners will have to understand passing etiquette.

One trick runners use on a long out-and-back, or one that involves night running, is to look behind you once in a while as you run. The trail can look very different from the opposite direction, so familiarizing yourself with both views can help you avoid getting lost on your return leg.

Point-to-Point

A point-to-point trail begins at one location and ends at another. In this case, runners are not likely to see others running in the opposite direction unless they are doubling back for a potty break! On a point-to-point run, racers will have to have a crew member drop them off at the starting line or meet them at the finish line.

Single-Track

A single-track trail is only wide enough for a single runner. Racing on a single track requires a good knowledge of etiquette and a heightened awareness of other runners, as traffic jams can occur, particularly at the beginning of a run.

Tackling Varied Terrain

The best way to tackle varied terrain is to practice. New runners will find hills really challenging, so find some hills and try them out. As you run, take mental notes. On the way up, which muscles are screaming? Did your stride and foot strike change? If so, how? Are you out of breath? How much of the hill could you handle before walking? On the way down, your observations may change. Did you lengthen your stride? Did gravity pull you downhill faster than your legs could carry you? Was it harder on your knees and ankles? Did your shoes have ample traction? After your run, think about your next hill challenge and set some new goals. Do you need a few days to rest before trying again? Do you want to add some treadmill work with varying elevation levels?

Try doing the same thing with sand, gravel, grass, mud, and even snow and ice. Don't avoid running in the rain! Running on wet ground poses different challenges than running on a dry path. Try obstacle running on trails with exposed tree roots, sharp rocks, streams, and deep crevasses. After a storm, you might even hear of a site where trees have fallen. What a great opportunity to try out something new—hurdling over trees! Just be careful.

Slow and Steady

As you experiment with various terrains, you will learn a few tricks. Firstly, go slowly with difficult patches. Particularly when you are training, there is no need for excessive speed. Focus on picking up your feet as you run. It's easy to start shuffling your feet or losing focus when you are confidently on your way on a smooth path, but these are natural trails, and a tree root, rock, or the tiniest debris can cause you to trip and fall if you are not paying attention. Increase your pace when you are on an easy segment, but exercise more caution on the tricky bits. You are not in this sport to learn how to face plant!

Shifting Focus

Find trails that offer a range of terrain rather than a consistent surface. This is important, as you need to train your brain to pivot quickly. Most runners develop the habit of visually focusing a few yards ahead rather than looking straight down. This gives the brain time to process the complexities ahead and adjust strategies. Sudden changes in pace or stride can cause a fall, so trail runners need to train their brains to be constantly alert to what is coming. Incidentally, looking ahead rather than down at your feet also improves your running posture.

It is also helpful to focus on more distant objects or landmarks when the going gets tough and tiredness sets in. Instead of thinking about the many miles to go, a strategic runner often looks ahead, finds a marker, maybe even a specific tree, and makes that the goal. Once the goal is met, it's off to another. Some runners even count steps when they feel their energy waning. They set a goal of just 50 steps more, then on to another 50.

Soon you will learn that your focus can change depending on your energy level. Immediately focusing on tricky terrain keeps you alert and safe. Focusing on a visible marker one hundred yards away can keep you going when you are drained. Focusing on a number of steps at a time can get you through the rough spots.

Weathering Weather

The weather will be a major consideration for the trail runner, and the first thing to remember is that this is not a sport for fair-weather folks. Be ready for everything from scorching heat to whiplashing rain and wind, and embrace the opportunity to train in every kind of situation. Embrace the pop-up downpour and look at it as a great cool-down. Breathe calmly through the humidity. Take it slower in fallen leaves, where you can't see the ground as clearly. Endure the wintery months and observe how the trails look and feel in the different seasons. I have run the same trails so many times, and I am still always amazed at how they change through the seasons.

Proper Gear is Your Best Friend

Clearly, your choice of gear is completely dependent on weather conditions. You'll need extra layers in the cold and potentially even on a mild day when you are accessing higher altitudes or confronted by wind. You'll need water-resistant gear when running in the rain or even in a humid environment. Always be thinking about the dangers of heat stroke and hypothermia, the discomfort of sunburn, and the threat of frostbite. I tend to keep sunscreen, bug spray, chaffing ointment, and a headlamp in my car at all times. It's great to know these are always available. If I show up to a trail and it's extra sunny, I can give myself a quick spray of sunscreen. If it rains and mosquitoes appear everywhere, I can quickly access bug spray and protect myself from nasty bites. Very importantly, if a run ends up taking a bit longer than anticipated or if I get started a bit late, having my headlamp in my car allows me to grab it and go. This way, I do not have to scrap the run because I'm not prepared.

Storms and Fog are Your Enemies

Checking weather forecasts prior to a training run or race is obviously smart, but experience will also teach you that weather conditions can change in a flash. Particularly at high altitudes, storms can arrive suddenly, afternoon temperatures can be much higher than the cool of early morning, and nightfall brings not only darkness but cold. A fairly common but potentially very dangerous scenario is a lightning storm. If you are unexpectedly caught outdoors and hear thunder, remember these tips:

- Find shelter as quickly as you can

- Immediately leave elevated areas

- Never shelter under a tree (trees can act as lightning rods, and lightning tends to strike tall objects)

- Move away from bodies of water, as water conducts electricity

- Be aware that lightning can start forest fires, so be alert for the smell, sound, and sight of smoke and flame.

Another potential weather threat is fog, whether it is a warm, marine-layer event or a gloomy, cold soup. Fog will increase the moisture content of the air and reduce visibility. Runners who have headlamps should turn them on—if you have one, a lower setting works better in the fog. Remember that runners can also hear one another, so talking, humming, whistling, or singing can alert others to your presence. If you do not have a headlamp, use the flashlight on your phone. Just remember that you are consuming power. Because your visibility is suddenly limited, slow down. You do not want to trip over hazards or lose the trail.

Some trail-running organizations partner with local Search and Rescue (SAR) teams to present seminars or YouTube broadcasts on emergency preparedness. This is a great way to learn tips for staying safe in any kind of situation. It's also a great idea to download applications that give you updates about local weather.

Navigating Trail Markings

National, state, and local parks may use different systems for marking hiking trails, but for the most part, communications on the trail will be clear. Signage will typically be permanent, affixed, and weatherproof. In the case of a trail closure, a runner might discover temporary messaging requesting that people stay off the trail completely or limit their visits to daylight or certain sections. In some situations, park rangers may also be available at nature centers to orient visitors to the environment. Other trails may even have self-guided QR code systems to help hikers learn about the unique features and hazards of a trail. Regardless of the case, pay attention to all signage and follow the directions of those whose job it is to keep you and the ecosystem safe. Please be particularly respectful of signage that declares an area a "sensitive habitat." We are so fortunate to have nature reserves that host species in need of our protection.

For a first-time racer, trail markings may be difficult to interpret, although run organizers are responsible for making their communications as clear as possible. Orienting yourself to a race prior to the start is essential. Some organizers produce a pre-race guide to the trail, explaining the precise markers to be used and showing photographs of some of their locations. Knowing what to look for before you start will save you a great deal of anxiety on the course.

Race markers can be made of various materials: affixed signs, brightly colored barrier tape (sometimes reflective), non-toxic spray paint or chalk, or flags. Markers will use arrows to indicate direction and dots or other symbols to indicate that runners are still on the right track. These are called affirmation marks. Markers are best placed at eye level or, where eye level is not possible, on the ground. So, in addition to watching for obstacles and hazards, the trail runner must be alert to the location of trail markers. Unlike a street marathon, where the herd is easy to follow and cheering crowds line the route, a trail runner, especially on an ultra, may be alone on the trail at times. It is therefore very important to know how to navigate the course independently. To ensure that you are never in a position to rely completely on someone else, do your research prior to the race and pack a compass and hard copy map. In the worst case, you will be able to go old-school to follow the trail.

Navigating at Night

On a very long run, racers will often need to continue at night. This poses a unique challenge in terms of locating trail markers. Hopefully, organizers will have chosen reflective materials, and the runners will wear headlamps. Keep in mind, though, that the tripping hazards on the trail will be harder to see, and if distracted for just a moment, the runner could easily miss a marker. In these situations, running with others in a pack is a really good strategy, as well as staying in communication by cell phone or radio.

What to Do if You Get Lost

Hopefully, a runner never gets disoriented or lost on the course, but accidents happen. Firstly, always remember to communicate your plans to someone prior to the run or race. Know how to contact a ranger if necessary. Pack emergency gear. If you truly feel lost, stop and think. Don't run any further. Depending on the circumstances, make a decision to move to an open area where you can get a better view of your surroundings or find a sheltered spot where you can stay warm and dry. If you are lost for a long period of time, in the dark, or exposed to bad weather, above all, stay calm and alert. Because you have communicated ahead of time, Search and Rescue teams will soon be out looking for you, and their work will be easier if you are not on the move. I was pacing a friend of mine at her first 100-mile race and prior to picking up her first pacer she unfortunately made a wrong turn and ended up lost. By her account, once she realized she was off course, she immediately stopped moving and took a moment to gather her thoughts and calm her fears. Then, she turned in the direction she came from and started looking for things she remembered seeing, like a log she had stepped over, a weirdly shaped tree, a rock formation, etc. She used these to slowly and carefully navigate her way back to the course, and while it was certainly frustrating to have gone two extra miles in such a long race, it was her focus and ability to remain calm in the situation that ultimately got her back on course and to the next aid station.

Prioritizing Safety While Navigating Challenging Conditions

In 2019, I set out to run the Banderas 100K. At the last minute, the course was changed due to flooding, and while it is amazing that they were able to pull off such a last-minute change, it really made things challenging. The Airbnb we had rented for the race was originally 15 minutes from the start but then became almost an hour away, so we had to prepare for more preparation time at the very last minute. Then, the course itself was one of the most technical I have ever experienced, with hills that required nose-to-knee type climbing tactics to get up them, single-track trails along ridges with very intimidating drop-offs, and just an overall sense of being in the middle of nowhere with absolutely no cell service. There was also a lot of dust being kicked up, making it an overall challenging experience. I ended up deciding to quit around mile 35 because I had stopped sweating hours prior and was clearly dehydrated. It was getting dark and harder to navigate the trail, and I started having issues with my breathing due to all the dust in the air. At that point, I had picked up my pacer, and she was running along with me and could see my strained breathing. She stopped me to talk about what to do. She was very honest and told me I had seven miles to go to the next aid station, or we could turn around and have about a two-mile walk back to the last aid station. It was a very hard decision to make, but given where I was and how I felt, we turned around. I still feel I made the right decision for my body and safety. It was a defeating walk to the previous aid station, and it is always hard to officially announce that you are pulling out of a race, but it was the best decision. There will always be other races, but you only have one body, so you have to take care of it. I can't say that I will ever go back to Banderas, but I will finish a 100K race.

Chapter 5:

Safety First: Staying Secure on

the Trails

Safety on the trail should always be a runner's primary concern. Accidents, injuries, exposure to difficult weather, disorientation, and fatigue are ever-present risks. The keys to avoiding these hazards are awareness and preparation.

Trail Preparedness

"Know before you go" is the perfect adage for the runner. Check the weather the day before you run and again the morning of the event. If there is any threat of a dangerous weather event, postpone or watch for cancellation announcements from the race organization. This means staying connected to social media communications that will deliver the latest updates. Research your trails. On training runs, check out new routes with buddies before you add them to your repertoire of training locations. During a race, read your pre-race manual and take note of the details that could help or hinder you. Pay particular attention to the locations of hydration stops, first aid stations, and bathrooms. Mark these on a hard copy map and think through how you could locate them in the dark if you had to. Instead of thinking, "I'll be fine," ask yourself, "What is the worst thing that can happen today?" Then, prepare for that scenario.

Make sure that you wear shoes and clothing appropriate for the altitude, weather, terrain, and time of day. Many runners have been protected by the right hat or jacket. Many a run has been ruined by forgetting sunscreen, sunglasses, a base layer, or long sleeves. Don't forget to pack extra socks in case you encounter a stream or wetland, and think about layers you may need to add as night falls or the day cools down.

Train carefully and gradually build up your strength and endurance before you attempt difficult terrain. No matter how tempting a particular course may be, if you are not ready for it physically, don't take it on yet. Arrogance and overconfidence will only yield setbacks. Be patient and work hard to get yourself into the ideal shape, and then tackle that trail. It will be worth the wait.

Above all, never head out on the trial without communicating with someone about your location, departure time, and estimated arrival time. As long as someone is expecting your return, someone will be ready to come find you if you run into trouble.

Packing Essentials

In addition to your well-chosen clothing, you will need a good pack for running. These vary from compact belt packs or specific hydration vests to full multi-day running backpacks. Your options will likely depend on the length of your run. The ideal pack should be lightweight, water-resistant, and, most importantly, comfortable. Waist or shoulder straps need to be padded, should fit snuggly so that they do not rub against your skin, and should be sufficiently wide to avoid digging into you. If you are training for long runs where you need to carry a pack with a significant load of equipment, don't forget to train with that pack on! NEVER try something new on race day! Not only will this help you learn to arrange the contents efficiently and adjust straps comfortably, but you will also become accustomed to the extra weight well before your event. Particularly prior to a race, check your pack carefully to make sure it is still in good condition. The last thing you need on a trail is a torn strap!

Determining what to carry will depend on the length of your run and the trail conditions. Be strategic. Think about water first, even for a short run. The fountain at the park isn't always working! With experience, figure out how much water you need for a long run. Ask yourself what would happen if you ran right past a hydration station in the dark, missing a fill-up. Calculate how much water you can actually carry. After 15 miles of running, that fluid feels very heavy. In the deep wilderness, carry a few water purification tablets. They are not heavy and have often saved a lost hiker's life.

Nutrition gels, chews, energy bars, and electrolyte drink mixes are typically lightweight, so pack a supply of these for a longer run. There are many of these products on the market, but not all of them are healthy, so do your research. Talk with your running community about what works best, and try out various flavors and textures before you head out on a long run. Many races provide nutrition products at hydration stations, but make sure you know what works for you before you pop something into your mouth. I have learned over the course of my ultra running that I cannot do gels for an extended period of time. After I hit a certain point in a race, if I am fueling with only gels, my stomach will reject everything, which, of course, is a worst-case scenario when trying to survive an ultra. However, while I no longer rely on gels and aim to eat from the aid station food selection to get my calories in, I always have a few gels in my pack in case I urgently need fuel. I know that my body can handle and appreciate a few gels along the way when necessary.

Emergency Supplies

Outdoor equipment stores will have lists of survival gear for hikers and sell a wide range of products. This is a great place to begin for a new trail runner. Just remember to minimize weight even more than a day hiker or an overnight backpacker would do. Nevertheless, don't sacrifice safety for speed.

Depending again on the length of your run and the terrain, pack extra batteries for your phone, a space blanket, a lighter, a headlamp, a whistle, a knife, and possibly a fire starter. Even the humble garbage bag can make a shelter if necessary.

First aid supplies are important too and might include bandages, athletic tape, antiseptic ointment, or hydrogen peroxide. If you take medications, pack an extra dose, just in case you become lost or delayed. An asthma inhaler, epinephrine needle, or antihistamine might be more specifically necessary for a runner with a serious condition.

Fortunately, many race organizers supply a kit list ahead of time, so you may have some help determining the contents of your pack. Be sure to unpack and resupply after an event. You really don't want to set out on the next run carrying soggy, stale energy bars, right?

Injury Prevention

The best way to prevent injuries is to train carefully and watch for overuse injuries. Every runner, however, will trip at some point on a trail. Hopefully, this will not result in any harm, except maybe a bruised ego. Wearing long pants and long sleeves will certainly help with a crash landing, and staying well away from steep drop-offs will prevent falling over a cliff. While on the trail, don't stop to back up and take a selfie! We often hear the tragic stories of hikers who go over a cliff doing just that.

Overuse injuries and tripping aside, you can minimize injuries by slowing down when you feel unstable. On a difficult uphill slope, especially a rocky one, slow down to a walk. On a downhill slope, be aware that your strides might be longer, and gravity might pull you down faster than your legs can carry you. In this case, just stop. If the angle is really steep, sidewind or cross over back and forth along the trail rather than heading straight down.

Experiment with taking smaller steps and lifting your feet higher when traversing terrain with lots of exposed roots or obstacles. Light feet can help with your agility.

Speaking of feet, prevent blisters by ensuring that your shoes fit well. When you do get blisters, keep the area clean and dry and allow them to heal before running again. If you develop calluses, leave them alone unless they are painful. Calluses are the body's way of toughening up skin exposed to friction. Take care of your toenails. Cut them short enough that they do not jam up against the ends of your shoes, but not so short that you cause ingrown toenails. Don't be surprised if you get runner's toe, a condition where the repeated pressure on the toe causes the nail to become discolored or even fall off. If this occurs painlessly, you might not need to worry, but painful or infected toenails need to be treated by a medical professional.

Communication Tools

In addition to your cell phone, there are some very impressive high-tech communication gadgets available. Of course, your budget will determine your purchases. Many trail runners collect an array of equipment over time, and technology constantly changes, so keep up with your research about what is available. Clearly, you are most likely going to carry your cell phone on a run. Remember, however, that phones run out of charge, rely on cell towers, can easily break with a fall, and older models are not waterproof if submerged. A GPS watch is a good alternative, and putting your phone on airplane mode when you are not actively using it can save on charge.

In the backcountry, a personal locator beacon (PLB) is a lifesaver, especially when cell phones fail. These lightweight, handheld devices transmit distress signals to satellite rescue systems. They also have lights built in for signaling in the dark. Like a cell phone, though, a PLB needs an electrical charge, so the runner must ensure that it is topped up. It is a one-way signaling system, so the user will not hear communications from a Search and Rescue (SAR) team and may require registration with a local emergency authority.

Satellite emergency notification devices (SENDs) can receive text messages and track the location of the user. Some versions can handle two-way communication and have features that confirm the receipt of messages. These can cost more than a PBL and can be heavier.

A trail runner without technology can also use simple techniques to communicate. A loud, sharp whistle not only alerts others to your location but can also deter wildlife. Three short blasts are an internationally recognized distress signal. A mirror can be used for visual signaling, as can a flashlight. The latter, however, can run out of charge.

If you have the opportunity, take a course in backcountry survival techniques or join a local Search and Rescue (SAR) organization. The skills you will learn may save a life—if not yours, a fellow runner's.

Navigation Know-How

Reading Maps and Using Compasses

Since a trail runner should be prepared for any contingency, practice reading maps and using your compass. Imagine what you would do on a long run if trail markers became obscured or were knocked down. This is when old-fashioned map reading comes in. You might use an electronic map that outlines your route, but you should also pack a hard copy. You will need to familiarize yourself with both prior to navigating the trail. This is particularly critical when you are in unfamiliar territory. You will get to know the landmarks, dips, and hills of your practice trails, but a new route may pose a challenge.

Be sure that whichever map you use is a topographical, or topo, map. These maps, sometimes also referred to as contour maps, indicate the elevations of the land as well as features and landmarks.

One of the major distinctions between electronic and traditional hard copy maps is that the former swivel as you move, so the road ahead always points forward. The built-in compass on your device shifts the angle of the map to orient it to your current position. A paper map, on the other hand, is stationary. The standard is that north should always be at the top of the page, so check to make sure your map is oriented correctly. With this kind of map, you must first locate north on a compass and then swivel the map yourself to align the top of the page with the compass. Both ways of reading maps take some practice, so be sure you've become competent before you head out. Perhaps the most important difference between the two maps is that the map attached to your cell phone or electronic device requires power. The beauty of a manual compass is that it is simple to use and needs no power source, so always carry one with you.

Using GPS

A handheld or watch Global Positioning System (GPS) device is also useful on the trail. There are many models and many communication features available, so these items can be costly. GPS devices can determine your location, including your altitude, and some can include compasses, cameras, maps, and SOS communication capability. Again, like a cell phone, a GPS device needs an electrical charge, so it can let you down if you are out of power. Learning to use a GPS consistently affords the trail runner one more safety feature.

Staying Oriented

The most important trick to staying oriented is staying alert. This can be challenging given the potentially distracting environments on the trail and the meditative state that runners often shift into. The mental focus every runner will need sharpens over time. This is why shorter runs and races are so valuable for novices. You will notice that with experience, you will naturally become more observant, registering small details that you might not have noticed before. This is your brain learning to remember the details of the course. As you train, you can hone this skill. On an early morning run to a nearby park, for example, plan to observe how many cars are in the lot. Count the stairs as you run up the staircase at the beach. When on a long run, make a mental note of forks in the trail, shifts in altitude, unusual rock formations, or vegetation. This way, in addition to having maps, compasses, and technology in your hands, you will have your own memory working for you. This is not so different than the experience we've all had when we park our car in a massive lot and return an hour later, having completely forgotten where we parked. If we had stopped for a few seconds to register the level, aisle, and lot signage, we'd never have lost track.

Knowing the Hydration and First Aid Stations

Naturally, staying oriented will get you to the finish line faster and reduce your chances of getting lost. Just as important is keeping an eye on the location of hydration and first aid stations, particularly during long or ultra runs. Knowing how long it is until the next opportunity to fill up on water, gels, or chews can help you ration the supplies you do have and help you hold out emotionally for a bit longer. This is also a great way to measure if you are still on course. If you know the next aid station is 5 miles from the previous one and you have gone 6 miles with no aid station in sight, odds are you are off course and need to begin back tracking to figure out where you missed a marker or made a wrong turn. If you experience a minor injury and cannot finish the run, you'll have to determine whether to go back to the last station or go forward to the next. In the case of a serious injury, you will need to call for help and be able to identify exactly where that help can locate you. Hopefully, this will never happen, but knowing ahead of time where stations are can certainly prevent or reduce issues.

Wildlife Encounters

Animals

Naturally, one of the most inviting features of outdoor trail running is, well, nature. When we are out in the wild, we need to remember to respect the native wildlife, not only for our safety but also to protect the creatures whose environment we are invading. Depending on the local ecosystem, a runner might encounter venomous snakes, coyotes, bobcats, wolves, deer, and even bears. Particularly during the summer months, we often hear tragic news about a hiker or tourist whose contact with wildlife ends with one or both being injured. Much of the time, this is avoidable with careful planning and a state of alertness.

The importance of orienting yourself to the trail prior to training or racing is critical. Please take the time to research your trail environment prior to heading out and prepare yourself accordingly. If you are in bear territory and its birthing season, consider taking some bear spray and carrying a noisemaker or airhorn. If there is a known activity level for nocturnal predators on your training trail, consider running during the daylight hours if you have that option. More importantly, if your chosen route is likely to put you or wildlife at risk, select a different location.

Regional, state, and national park trails have signage indicating the presence of wildlife species. Typically, this signage also indicates the seasonality and traits of various species, so pay attention to the posted information. If you are in rattlesnake territory, know the habits of your slithering friends and be on the lookout. It's easy to slip into a distracted or meditative state of mind while running, but it only takes one wrong step to invite a bite. If you are meandering through little piles of coyote scat, remember that there are tricksters nearby, even if you cannot see or hear them. Don't forget to use your eyes and your ears, and stay aware.

Equally important, please respect the animal life on the trail. Remember that you are invading their natural space, not vice versa. Think of yourself as an honored guest and use your trail running as an opportunity to enhance local conservation efforts. Remember that these animals are simply protecting their homes and their families, just as we protect ours. Be respectful and stay away from babies, no matter how adorable they are. Many wildlife attacks happen when runners get too close to an animal's babies, so be respectful and mind their space. Stay on the designated trail, avoid unnecessary noise pollution, and don't leave anything behind except wonderful memories.

Insects

While we often think about risky run-ins with animal life in the outdoors, we should also remember that even little pests can create big problems. Mosquitos, black flies, wasps, spiders, scorpions, and ticks present various challenges and require different avoidance strategies, so remember to research the insect life before you embark. It is important to know your environment!

Many issues can be prevented by choosing appropriate clothing: long sleeves, long pant legs, pant legs tucked into socks, tall socks when wearing shorts to protect your ankles, repellant fabrics, light colors, hats, etc. Avoid perfumes, lotions, or scented sunscreens, which could attract bees.

If possible, avoid peak hours for certain insects. Mosquitos, for instance, tend to come out in force after sunset. Never reach under rocks, into holes, or anywhere you cannot see who might be lurking there. No doubt you will learn from experience that if you run with your mouth wide open while passing through a cloud of gnats, you will surely eat some! Above all, stay on the path, preferably towards the center if you aren't near other runners, and keep away from foliage, long grasses, and brushy areas where little bugs might be hiding out.

If you do experience an insect bite or sting while on a trail run, be prepared with first aid. Acquaint yourself with first-aid remedies ahead of time so you know how to respond. It's also important to shower after every outside run and check your skin and clothing for indications of insect bites or stings. Ticks present a particular risk as they can carry Lyme disease, so complete tick checks with a partner and learn how to remove ticks safely. Of course, prior to applying any specific first-aid remedies, clean insect bites or sting sites with soap and water.

Plant Life

In her infinite wisdom, Mother Nature has a wealth of protective strategies in her hands. Animals and insects might stand out as obvious risks on the trail, but knowledge of hazardous plant life is equally important, as many plants contain ingenious defensive mechanisms.

Obviously, the first rule of the road is to never ingest any plant material found on the trail, even if you believe you've identified a friendly berry or two. No one wants to try to complete a run while dealing with nausea, cramps, or diarrhea!

There are also many plant species that contain toxic oils or piercing needles. Those who have had unfortunate encounters with poison oak, poison ivy, and cactus know that these culprits are frequent residents of the trail environment. Lesser-known species like poison sumac, deadly nightshade, stinging nettle, foxglove, monkshood, and giant hogweed can also contain toxins, causing reactions ranging from discomfort to serious illness.

Inevitably, every trail runner will brush against all kinds of plant life. After all, you are in the midst of it! So, the prevention of injury and illness is key. Just as parks post signage about local wildlife, they typically also post warnings and photographs regarding hazardous plants. Learn what these plants look like and where they are usually located. Download a plant identification application on your phone, and as you discover new trails, make a study of the surrounding flora. Talk to other runners to see what they've experienced and learn from them.

Conservation Hack

Take some time to complete an interpretive program or orientation with a park ranger or warden. What a wonderful byproduct of your new trail running sport! You'll soon become a conservationist, perhaps volunteering with a local trail maintenance team. A National Directory of Trail Maintenance Organizations can be found on the American Trail Running Association's (ATRA) website.

A Word About Running Solo

Although a certain peace comes from running alone and completely immersing yourself in the natural environment, it's never a good idea to be out solo in the wilderness. Quite simply, too many risks are present. Nature can be a beast, which is why humans live in social communities. While it may be safe to run by yourself on a groomed trail in the local park, there are also potential hazards there. It's sad to say, but one such hazard is crime. I've turned a corner in a nearby ecological reserve to encounter a pop-up encampment with drunk, rowdy men. I've also been on a trail clean-up event where we located a stash of drug paraphernalia. From time to time, we hear stories of tragic abductions of innocent joggers. If you have no alternative to a solo run, choose a route through a well-populated park. You are less likely to encounter danger if you are surrounded by families setting up birthday parties! Better still, run with a buddy. In either case, invest in pepper spray, know how to use it, and keep your cell phone charged and handy. Think about taking a self-defense class like Krav Maga, the Israeli practice where the driving concept is "if anyone is getting home safely today, it is me". The additional confidence and fitness you can gain from such a discipline will enhance your runs too.

"The miracle isn't that I finished. The miracle is that I had the courage to start."
– John Bingham

This book is all about unlocking the magic of trail running and conquering ultramarathons. My hope is to help beginners find their way in the world of ultrarunning, just like I did.

Now that you are halfway through, I want to ask if you would also like to help someone just starting out and in need of guidance? Your review on this book could be the light at the end of the trail for them. It costs nothing and takes less than a minute, but it could make a huge difference in someone's ultrarunning journey.

Your thoughts could support:

- A newbie runner's first steps towards adventure.
- Someone dreaming of running an ultramarathon.
- A trail runner seeking guidance and inspiration.

Simply scan the QR code to leave your review:

Thank you from the depths of my heart for being part of this journey. Looking forward to sharing more exciting adventures and running strategies in the book. Let's continue exploring the trails together!

Best wishes,
Sarah Russell

Chapter 6:

Nutrition and Hydration:

Fueling Your Trail Adventures

The Trail Diet

Because of the heavy caloric burn that runners experience, their nutritional needs will differ from those of the average person. High energy needs, muscle repair, bone density, and even mental awareness depend a great deal on your day-to-day diet. Like any health-conscious individual, runners need to pay attention to macronutrients (protein, carbohydrates, and fats) and micronutrients (vitamins and minerals). Whether a runner is on the Mediterranean or Keto diet, or is a pescatarian, vegetarian, or vegan, appropriate dietary habits are fundamental to the general health of an athlete.

A vital aspect of a runner's everyday lifestyle is water intake. Although various medical organizations differ slightly on their recommendations for daily water intake, typical suggestions are between 10 and 11 cups for adult women and between 12 and 15 cups for adult men. This does not take into consideration weather, body weight, age, or activity level, so the individual athlete should calculate the ideal amount needed given those factors.

The National Agricultural Library of the United States Department of Agriculture has a collection of well-researched resources identifying the nutritional needs of humans. When it comes to figuring out how many macros and micros a runner needs on a daily basis, there is so much to know. Firstly, athletes need more protein than non-athletes, and runners will need even more protein when exercising more intensely. Age, gender, body weight, and type of diet all play a part in determining nutritional needs. Since there are so many factors to consider as you enter the trail running world, seek expert advice, talk with your coaches and colleagues, and most importantly, listen to your body. You will dream of steak if you need it!

Macronutrients

Protein

Protein is the key building block for muscle, so all athletes need to be highly aware of their protein intake. Not only do runners need to build muscle, but they also need to repair muscle after every workout. This is also why rest days are so crucial. Runners and other serious athletes need to consume more protein than sedentary or less active individuals because they are constantly in a state of body repair. A lack of protein intake will eventually result in slow muscle repair and fatigue. A long-term protein deficiency can even result in much more serious conditions: hair loss, exhaustion, muscle loss, and injury.

This does not mean the ultra runner should wolf down grease-soaked burgers every day, although cravings for this kind of food can certainly result from a protein deficiency! Lean protein, or, in other words, protein low in fat, are the healthiest. Examples might be eggs, poultry, fish, and tofu. Vegetarians and vegans, however, face a unique challenge. While they require the same amount of protein as meat eaters, they must combine non-animal protein sources, such as beans and rice, in order to create complete proteins. Learning what to put together, when, and in what quantities can be a bit of a study.

Carbohydrates

According to Johns Hopkins' Runner's Diet, carbohydrates should make up 60–70% of a runner's consumption, while protein and healthy fat should make up 15–20%. Carbs are found in blood glucose, which delivers immediate energy to the body through the circulation system, and in glycogen, which is stored in the liver and muscles for later use. A deficit in carbs will result in a deficit in energy and, ultimately, in a bonk, or sudden loss of energy (Eidel, 2022).

Fruits, vegetables, and whole grains are healthy carbohydrates. Chips and donuts—well, we know they are not the best choices! As you gain experience with your nutrition and your runs, you may realize that certain carbohydrates can cause more gastrointestinal distress than others. Too much flatulence during a race does not create jet propulsion, but it may create stomach discomfort.

Fats

Fats are the third macronutrient and are equally important to the diet. We do need to differentiate, though, between healthy and unhealthy fats. Nuts and seeds, dairy products, egg yolks, fish, and many vegetable oils are all sources of healthy fat. Fats categorized as saturated and trans fats, which are often found in deep-fried or processed foods, should be avoided. Runners who make a habit of reading nutritional labels will soon become highly aware of and careful of how they are fueling their bodies.

Micronutrients

The many vitamins and minerals required for your body to function well are just as important as the macronutrients. Calcium, vitamin B12, vitamin C, vitamin D, and iron are commonly associated with healthy bones, skin, and hearts. The study of micronutrients is so technical that once again, beginning runners should engage in deep research and consult sports medicine experts about the ideal make-up of these components. Every athlete should have a physical examination each year and should request that a blood panel be completed. Discussing the elements of a blood test with a medical practitioner will provide a runner with up-to-date information about any nutritional deficiencies. A few years back, I had just come off of a 50 mile race and was suddenly becoming lightheaded and nauseous during easy low mile runs. So I decided to go see my physician and have my blood panel completed. It turned out my body was severely lacking iron, which was causing the fatigue and dizziness. The doctor recommended some simple over the counter iron supplements and after a few weeks I was feeling much better. Sometimes it is a very easy fix, but if not addressed or managed it can lead to some scary consequences.

Hydration

If there is one absolute that every trail runner must swear by, it is the need for ample, clean water. This is why one of the initial gear recommendations is a hydration system, and this is why hydration stations are present at every racing event. Although we know that life can be maintained for a while with no or little food, the human body cannot survive without water for long. The volume of water needed during a training session or during a race will depend on the runner's physical profile (age, gender, body weight, etc.), the length of the run, and the weather. At extreme temperatures—blizzards and very high heat, for instance—runners should simply postpone. Dehydration in the heat or even in the dry cold is very dangerous and can result in heat exhaustion, heat stroke, or even death. Even if you have trained hard and looked forward to an event for months, pushing yourself in the heat is never safe.

Most competitors water up several hours prior to a race and then hydrate regularly, sipping water every 15 minutes or so. They frequently comment that the best approach is to drink before thirst sets in. Yes, of course, your body will signal that you need water, but when you are racing, your system could already be under considerable stress before you feel thirst. Sipping a little every now and then is preferable to chugging down a gallon of water after you are parched. Chugging water, by the way, is sure to give you a belly ache.

In addition to water, our bodies need electrolytes, the minerals in our body fluids responsible for chemical reactions and electrical charges. These minerals include calcium, chloride, magnesium, phosphorus, potassium, and sodium. We lose electrolytes through urination and sweating, but we can replace them quickly with electrolyte-infused sports drinks and gels. Some runners take salt pills during ultra runs to avoid a serious loss of electrolytes.

An electrolyte deficiency can be quite dangerous, so runners need to be aware of the warning signs: nausea, dizziness, cramps, and exhaustion. Conversely, too many electrolytes in the system can produce similar symptoms, which is equally concerning. The goal should be balance. Learning your body's unique needs and listening to its complaints will help you find this balance.

As odd as it may seem, a great way to tell if you are not sufficiently hydrated, or even overhydrated, is the color of your urine. Yes, we are talking about pee here. If you use the restroom before, during, or after a run and your pee is a very dark yellow or even brownish, it is a sign that you are very dehydrated and need to step up your hydration game quickly. Similarly, you can actually be overhydrated. Overhydration, while it sounds like a good thing, unfortunately flushes out your electrolytes faster and can cause an imbalance that will make you feel nauseous, dizzy, and tired. Therefore, if your urine is clear, you may want to pull back on your water consumption, or at the very least, step up your electrolyte game with a salt tablet or gel. When using color as your guide, you should be aiming for a very pale-yellow urine color. This means you are at the perfect balance of hydration, which, on extreme heat or exertion days, can be very hard to maintain, but do your best and try to be mindful of what your body needs. It will always benefit you in the long run.

Pre-Run Diet

Many marathoners and ultra runners follow the practice of carb loading 24–48 hours prior to a long race in order to maximize their energy reserves and reduce the possibility of fatigue. Ideal foods are low in fiber and fat and include choices like fruit or fruit juice, potatoes, white bread, rice, and pasta. Right before a strenuous event, runners should avoid foods that are spicy, difficult to digest, and unfamiliar. Foods high in fiber can cause gas, bloating, and cramps, so choices like oatmeal, beans, and bran may be healthy, but just not before a run! Many also avoid caffeine just prior to a race so they can concentrate on running to the finish line rather than running to the bathroom.

A light carbohydrate-based meal two or three hours prior to a run or a light snack 30 minutes beforehand can also help raise your energy levels right before an event. It's also important to hydrate before a run, but without drinking too much.

Many new runners look at carb loading as an opportunity to eat whatever they want and overindulge. I certainly did when I first started out. In reality, overeating the night before is never the best option and can cause you to feel heavy and weighed down on your run. Very often, this can lead to some yucky stomach issues along the way as your body works to process the overload of food while also trying to keep you moving forward. Eat a normally sized meal and focus on finding food that your body can digest easily and that has a higher carbohydrate content than your average daily meals.

Eating on the Go

This is by far the hardest part of training. Everyone's body is different, and what works for me may not work for you, and vice versa. Unfortunately, it's a lot of trial and error, but once you find what works for you, it is amazing to see what your body can really do. In truth, it took me about three years to really perfect my on-the-go eating. Prior to figuring it out, there were several races when I dealt with stomach issues, dizziness, nausea, exhaustion, etc. During many of them, I was still able to compete, but I always had a constant desire to figure out the ideal approach because I knew if I got my food intake right, I would be unstoppable.

Trail-friendly snacks are those that resupply the body quickly with energy and are easy to manage and hold down while you keep moving. It's not unusual to feel some nausea when your body is in a state of exertion, so consuming calories before this sets in and also avoiding overloading are equally important. Learning what to eat, when, how often, and how much will come with experience. Most long-distance runners will not need to fuel up during a run shorter than an hour or so, but even short runs can be an opportunity to experiment with what works best for your body in terms of snacking on the run.

The most typical choices for fueling while running are electrolyte-infused or energy drinks, energy gels and chews, which contain carbohydrates and electrolytes, and light snacks like bananas. There is an entire niche market for products specifically designed for long-distance events; you will see them on display tables at running events, find them in your registration packet, and receive them from friendly race volunteers en route or at nutrition and hydration stations. Know ahead of time what works for you, so you don't have any issues mid-race. There are also many sports nutrition products inaccurately labeled or advertised as healthy. We've all seen a granola bar loaded with refined sugars and high in the wrong kinds of fat! Study the nutrition labels on various products so you can make good choices.

Snacking on an ultra trail run requires even more preparation than you might need during an urban marathon, where volunteers line the entire route and constantly hand you snacks. On the trail, you will need to carry your own supplies, so you must be strategic about weight and convenience. Unwrapping a soggy peanut butter sandwich while trying to race up a hill might be a challenge, and if you don't have ample water to wash it down, well, that's another problem! Take fuel you can manage with one hand, minimize trash, as you will have to carry it to the next rest stop, and please never litter. Wrappers, peels, or remnants of food are not only harmful to the environment but could also mess up the trail for other runners. So, think ahead and be practical when you snack on the trail.

Another great hack for running an ultra is to always have something, either with you or with your crew, that you know will sound good to you. Under duress, our bodies will begin to fight against taking in the nutrients we need. You may roll up to an aid station, and everything you look at turns your stomach.

Nothing sounds good, but you know you have to put something in your body. I have found that having a special treat saved away will usually do the trick. It doesn't even have to be something healthy, but do try to make it something that gets you proteins, calories, sugar, and/or salt—all foods that get into the body quickly and provide energy. Try something like a Snickers bar that has nuts for proteins and salt and chocolate for sugar.

Post-Run Recovery

Remember that peanut butter sandwich? It's a great post-run recovery food! Within an hour or so after a run, you will want to refuel with a combination of protein and carbohydrates, so peanut butter is now your hero. The protein component will be key for rebuilding your muscles, while the carbs will restore the energy reserves.

It is very common for runners, particularly after a long run, to lack appetite. Their bodies are cooling down from a period of exertion, so they are not concentrating immediately on eating. Nevertheless, it's important to replace those calories strategically. Consuming a heavy meal after an ultra is likely to cause discomfort, so begin slowly with a calorie-dense but light meal or snack. Protein shakes, eggs, fruit, or a sandwich are all good choices. Wait a few hours before eating a celebratory meal.

You will also want to be very cautious about alcohol consumption post-run. No doubt you have trained hard and long for an event and will be swept up in the euphoria of the finish line. You'll be very tempted to celebrate! Please keep in mind that your body has been highly stressed and is now entering a recovery phase. You may even be dehydrated but unaware of it. If you have an alcoholic drink, make sure you balance it with healthy foods, water, and electrolytes.

Understand also that a recovery period may not be a single evening or even one to two days. Particularly after an ultra, and depending, of course, on your unique needs, it may take your system several days or even weeks to recover. You will need time, sleep, and calories to replenish your glycogen reserves and repair muscle. Don't be surprised if you've incurred minor injuries like blisters, stressed tendons, or pulled muscles, so don't rush your return to the trail. Recommit to your everyday, healthy nutritional practices and pamper your body a little until you have rested up.

Coming Back From a Bonk

My coach and I joke a lot about bonks during races and out on longer training runs. On one of my 50-mile races, I went from sailing through aid stations for the first 20+ miles all smiles, then coming into the 25-mile aid station in tears because everything hurt and I didn't feel good. My coach told me to remember the difference between hurt and hurting and asked me if I was hurt. I wasn't; I was hurting. She got me to take in some much-needed calories and hydration and sent me on my way. This was tough love, but exactly what I needed in that moment. It's ok to feel emotional during these runs; in fact, it's completely normal because you are working your body at a level most people can't even imagine. By the next aid station, I was back to smiling and feeling much better; I just needed to have that moment to get the fuel and mindset adjustment I needed to keep going. I ended up not only finishing the 50 miles when I wanted to quit at 25, but also setting a personal record. The important thing to focus on is knowing whether you are hurt or hurting. Running longer distances is going to be painful, and you're going to experience cramps and random pains that pop out of nowhere and then magically disappear. Your feet and legs will hurt, but the feeling at the end of the race will be worth pushing through the pain. This is hurting, but being hurt is a different story. If you get hurt during your race or run, don't try to push through the pain like I did when I stress-fractured my knee. Yes, I finished that marathon, but because of the damage I did running 26.2 miles with a stress fracture, I was completely out of commission for eight months. That one race wasn't worth all the time I missed on the trail.

Chapter 7:

Mind Over Trail: Mastering the Mental Game

There is absolutely no argument that trail running, like any rigorous endurance sport, is physically demanding. We know that gear, training, good nutrition, regular hydration, and practical recovery strategies work together to make the physical challenge possible.

Any runner knows that your mental game is sometimes even more critical. It takes confidence and a good dose of humility to begin any new endeavor, especially when you are on the novice's learning curve. Discipline is required when you are tired or simply feeling unmotivated to go for that run. You need a good reserve of grit to push ahead through all kinds of tough terrain and weather. Finally, optimism and courage will give you strength when recovering from an injury that sets you back or forces you to adapt to new limitations or goals. Developing confidence, humility, discipline, grit, optimism, and courage is a magical recipe not only for success on the trail but also for success in life.

Mental Agility

Running ultras requires one kind of strategic training, while shorter, faster races require another. Effective training plans can require complex workout schedules, and trail terrain requires quick thinking. Clearly, trail running requires mental agility as well as physical agility. Like any serious athlete, a trail runner will need to develop a great deal of mental flexibility. Perhaps you have planned your weekend around completing a long run, but then a heat wave makes a sudden appearance. You may arrive at your chosen trail to find out it has been flooded and closed for maintenance. We often talk about work-life balance. For runners, it's even more complex: the work-life-training balance. For those with young families, it may be the work-life-childcare-training balance. Remaining consistent with workouts and training often requires pivoting quickly from plan A to plan B without becoming frustrated.

Mental agility is even more crucial on the trail. Should you try to run up that hill or climb up and save energy for the remaining miles? It's getting dark; should you call it a day or push through to complete that extra section of trail? There's a fallen tree ahead; should you go over or around? Every second of the run requires decision-making. This is where trail running is so different from mindlessly pounding the pavement, but it is certainly why trail running is much more fun. A trail runner is constantly scanning the upcoming terrain and calculating the next move, rather than looking down at the ground. The mental focus required by the sport precludes it from ever becoming boring.

Much of your mental agility will come from setting realistic, attainable goals and then being able to quickly change the strategies that move you towards those goals. You may have to give up or change a workout, or even cancel the running camp you were looking forward to, but you don't have to give up the long-term goal of running the ultra. Consistency in training does not mean you work out on the same day or at the same time each week. The need for a rest day sneaks up on you, believe me! Redefine consistency as your ability over time to keep up your training and incrementally add weight or reps to your strength workout, miles to your run, or skills to your yoga routine.

Before long, you may even notice that the mental flexibility you have developed for your sport seeps into every aspect of your life. Building elasticity in your lifestyle and learning that all great plans need constant revision will make you a stronger and more confident person.

Emotional Resilience

A bit earlier I mentioned the time in 2019 I crewed and paced one of my best friends (and coach) on her first 100-mile race. We had mapped everything out prior to race day and had an Excel spreadsheet we used to predict her arrival at each aid station. We could even update that spreadsheet on the fly using my laptop (I tend to be a bit of a tech nerd and have a love for Excel). She started out strong and was crushing miles through most of the first half with very few issues or setbacks, and she was certainly coming into aid stations either as expected or faster. Later in the day, though, as the sun started to set and the temperatures started to drop, we were waiting for her at the next aid station, where she had planned to pick up a pacer to help push her along on the challenging back half of the race. We waited and waited, talking ourselves out of worrying and telling ourselves that she probably just slowed down a little since it was getting dark. However, runner after runner came through our aid station, and she was nowhere to be seen. We had the race monitors radio back to the previous aid station, and they were able to tell us when she left. The numbers just weren't adding up.

Naturally, we began to worry. The temperatures were still dropping, and this was the station where we had planned to change her clothes and get her into something warmer for running during the night. Finally, quite a while after anticipated, she came into the station freezing, upset, and very discouraged. She had gotten off trail at some point and ended up going almost a mile off course before she realized it and had to trace back her steps and find the path again. This was terrifying for her, as she was alone, and it was very dark at this point. Our first step was to immediately address her clothing needs. She was shivering and near hypothermia due to the massive temperature drop, sweating, and a few soggy creek crossings. We got her completely changed and started to warm her up, and then we had to address the mental disappointment and get her ready to head back out. She was discouraged, frustrated with herself and the course, and, naturally, tired. But her team was not going to let her give up! Fortunately, this was the aid station where she had arranged to pick up a pacer, so we were able to assure her she would never be alone as she finished her race. We divided up the remainder of the course between myself and two other pacers to get her to the finish line. In a true show of grit, determination, and mental and emotional resilience, she not only finished her first 100-mile race, but she was also the first female finisher...even with the two-mile journey off course.

Developing mental agility goes hand-in-hand with building emotional resilience. A life of trail running will present emotional obstacles as well as physical pitfalls and roadblocks. Having a natural tendency for patience is a wonderful asset, but runners tend to be can-do, ambitious people who jump into challenges with little hesitation. Understanding ahead of time that there will be difficult moments is a huge part of the practice.

Resilience on the actual trail is built with experience. Unlike a traditional marathon, where a runner can plan for the crowds, the curves in the road and the inevitable hills will confront a trail runner with surprises. Maintaining a positive attitude when the going gets rough is sometimes easier said than done. In the face of rain and cold, scrapes and bruises, or losing the trail markers, a runner will have to fight discouragement and press on. Runners who learn to expect the difficulties and see them as growth opportunities will soon thrive. That steep hill that just appeared ahead—no problem! Oh, a muddy marsh! What a lovely opportunity to cool off! With time, minor injuries, faster racers passing by, and embarrassing stumbles will bring out the warrior spirit. When a runner embraces a disappointing performance as a learning experience rather than as a failure, the next challenge becomes even easier to conquer.

There are moments, however, when the emotional load becomes too heavy. Some runners experience depression following a race, and it's no surprise. They may have prepared for and dreamed of the event for months, potentially years. Suddenly, the excitement they anticipated is over. Even if they have a fantastic result, there is bound to be a period of anticlimax during the recovery period. Many racers find that the antidote to this phenomenon is registering for another event and establishing a new training plan.

A serious injury, similarly, can create a very difficult emotional crisis. Imagine you have trained vigorously and enthusiastically anticipated race day, only to be injured before the event. Not only will you miss the long-awaited moment, but you may be laid up for weeks or months. You may even require surgery or physical therapy. Add to that the loss of the emotional high that comes with exercise. Nothing is more difficult for active athletes than forced passivity. Ideally, after a very forgivable but limited pity party, a runner with emotional resilience will think through a new plan. If you can't run for six months, what can you do? Can you take up swimming, try aqua-aerobics, or rent a rowing machine? Can you kick up the strength training or master Tai Chi? If there are moments when your running future looks bleak, a sports psychologist or running coach can also provide new insights. You may feel like you have taken an enormous step backwards when you can now only walk-run a mile, but remember, you are back in the game. That's the win.

It's not easy, but thinking of a limitation as an opportunity to try something different can open exciting new doors. We should never forget that there are many who have struggled with similar or worse disappointments; sometimes the inspiration of heroic athletes with permanent disabilities can really help us climb out of a slump. Just as our physical and mental agility spill over into all aspects of our lives, the emotional resilience gained from overcoming disappointment will build unbeatable character.

Mindful Running

Mindful running is something everyone can practice. It entails entering a state of enhanced focus on your current surroundings and your body. This is perhaps the most addictive aspect of the sport, as it allows us to absorb the beauties of the natural world and, at the same time, escape from the stresses of everyday life. Many experienced runners report that they begin to notice nuanced details of their breathing, stride, or small muscle movements—details they would not normally perceive.

The benefits of mindful running are akin to the benefits of meditation. In fact, many runners consider their moments on the trail meditative and report lowered stress levels, better sleep quality, and improved blood pressure.

There are a few pointers to developing and practicing a mindful approach to running: run outside; run without distractions like watches, music, audiobooks, or conversation (i.e., no cell phone or headphone!); pay attention to one body part at a time and let it speak to you; think about your breathing and your heartbeat and how they work together; observe fluctuations in your pace, stride, and foot strike as you work through the changing elements of the trail; and finally, stop thinking about your mileage and your time. Notice if you are tensing up your shoulders or holding back your stride, and then work on releasing those tensions and taking note of the changes to your speed, stride, and overall sensation while running. Allow yourself the luxury of completely immersing your mind in the environment and the workings of your body.

Other than stress relief, the most obvious benefit of running this way is to sharpen the relationship between your body and your conscious mind. You may become more aware of physical stresses before they become injuries. You may find that you learn to run even more strategically as you listen to your body. You will soon find that mindfulness is a habit that seeps into all aspects of your life.

Unsurprisingly, many athletes enter the world of trail running because of the competitive aspects of the sport. We humans love the opportunity to build our emotional strength by setting and meeting tough challenges. However, adding sessions of mindful running to those more intense workouts or events where the goal is simply speed or endurance will benefit the whole you!

Overcoming Obstacles

If there were ever a sport that presented constant obstacles, it would be trail running. Physical, mental, and actual obstacles are the elements of the sport that you can count on. A good approach, then, is to assume that those obstacles are coming at you.

Often, this kind of thinking entails purposefully deciding to see your experiences differently and practicing that mindset. I've had many days when my goal was to make a certain time or distance, but I just didn't have the juice to finish. I could choose to see that run as a failure, or I could give myself kudos for simply showing up. Disciplining yourself to see the disappointments as wins develops resilience. Did an injury cause a pity party and tempt you to quit, or did it build your resolve? Did you creatively figure out a new training plan with recovery in mind and learn that setting new goals is a reset, not a failure? Maybe at this particular moment in time, building character was more important than extending mileage.

Athletes from every serious sport learn the same lesson. There are going to be some very tough times: superior competitors, physical exhaustion, interrupted training schedules, discouragement, and literal and metaphorical bumps in the road. They also learn that pushing through the obstacles rather than avoiding them builds the inner strength that you'll need to withstand the bumps and bruises of life in general.

The Pain Cave vs Bonking

The "Pain Cave" is a rite of passage for every trail runner. It is the point in a difficult run when you start asking yourself, "What the heck am I doing to myself?" and "Why am I tormenting my body like this?" Ultra runners comment that they expect to enter the Pain Cave at some point, so they prepare emotionally ahead of time and try to take a bring-it-on approach. They often mention that running into and through this stage teaches them that they can stretch their limits if they have the will. In this sense, the Pain Cave can ultimately be very empowering.

Most ultra runners have also experienced bonking, but unlike the Pain Cave, this state cannot be resolved with sheer will. Bonking, or sudden energy crashing, is very unpleasant, highly discouraging, and potentially dangerous. Bonking is caused by low blood sugar resulting from insufficient fuel and is characterized by overall weakness, nausea, fatigue, dizziness, and potentially even disorientation. Bonking is much more serious than simply feeling tired, so if you feel this state coming on, you need to pause your run, get assistance, refuel and hydrate your body, and rest until you have recovered. Hopefully, you will be able to resume your run, but this can also take several days. If you experience this state repeatedly, you should seek medical attention to find out whether something more serious is going on.

Finding Flow

By now, you'll have seen that finding your flow is about entering a mental zone of heightened awareness. The term "flow" was originally coined by a Hungarian psychologist, Mihaly Robert Csikszentmihalyi, in the 1970s. Concentration on the moment, self-awareness, connecting action with awareness of that action, and the feeling of empowerment are all components of the flow state. Those who lose themselves in painting, gardening, yoga, and, of course, trail running, are experiencing flow.

Paradoxically, runners tend to find flow when they slow down. This doesn't necessarily mean slowing down the pace of the run; it means slowing down thought. We are so conditioned to multi-tasking, filling our days with frenzied activities, and trying to cheerfully juggle family, work, chores, and social obligations. Flow doesn't happen when we frenetically toggle back and forth between competing thoughts. It doesn't occur when we are constantly checking our race time or trying to outpace a competitor. Nor does flow set in while we are running on the treadmill, watching the television in front of us and listening to music at the same time. Flow occurs when we still our minds and simply focus on the workings of our bodies in the here and now. The rhythm of running and the calming effect of the outdoor environment lend themselves to this mental state.

Practicing meditation, belly breathing, yoga, or forest bathing may sound like a 1960s hippie revival, but there are plenty of healthy folks who recognize that these activities produce a state of flow that results in an overall improvement in wellbeing. Runners who consciously aim to reach that state during training find that they soon become adept at shifting into the flow state, even in their non-running hours.

Overcoming Mental Blocks During a Grueling Trail Race

My second-ever 50K was, by far, my most grueling race. I took on this race only two weeks after my very first 50K (not recommended!). I was new to the sport and thought two weeks was plenty of time for my body to recover and be ready to do it again. It was not. This was a looped course (two loops, each a little over 15 miles). I completed the first loop alright—not great—and my body was already tired, but I still had the motivation and just enough energy to take off for the second loop. This is where things got messy. I started feeling dizzy and nauseous from a lack of hydration, electrolytes, and food in general, and my body was simply not in peak condition from the beginning. I was barely making it through the aid station cutoffs and was walking a lot by the midpoint of the second loop. I was frustrated, discouraged, and overwhelmed. I finally came up to the very last aid station prior to the finish (about 2.5 miles from the finish line). I was in rough shape: I had stopped sweating, was very dizzy, and was slightly unaware of where I was, which is a sign of exhaustion and very risky. But I was new to the sport and stubborn, and I told myself to keep going. After all, it was only two miles to go. I left the aid station pretending all was well in order to make sure the aid station helpers didn't pull me from the course. As I set out, the situation only got worse. It was only two more miles, but mentally and physically, those were the longest, most grueling two miles of my life. At one point, I felt so terrible that I sat down on a rock slightly off the trail and out of the way and just cried. I was falling apart. I vaguely remember taking in a gel and some more water to wash it down and immediately feeling like it was all going to come right back up. Thankfully, it didn't. I spent several minutes sitting there, upset and overwhelmed, knowing that I had to keep moving. So, I allowed myself one more minute to cry and let out everything I was feeling, and then I told myself that after one minute was up, I would stand and go finish the race.

In the end, that's just what I did. I let it all out for 60 seconds, stood up, and started walking towards the finish. I told myself in that moment that even if I had to walk two miles, I would not stop, and I would just keep moving towards the finish line. I finished that 50K dead last, but guess what? Someone's got to do it! I was actually proud. I didn't care that I was last or that they were putting away the tables at the finish line, and the only people there to cheer me through were my family. If anything, that made it even better. I knew that I had given that race everything I had, both mentally and physically, and the people I care about the most were there to see it! I tell this story not to encourage anyone to take on two races way too close together and suffer through it, because in truth, it was not a safe choice and my situation could have been dire. I tell that story to encourage you not to give up when your head gets in the way. These types of races bring out all kinds of emotions along the way, and the key is to learn how to talk yourself through those tough times. What can you tell yourself to get yourself moving? Is it consciously giving yourself 60 seconds to "let it all out"? Is it a mantra that you can repeat to yourself, or maybe a song you can sing in your head to distract you and make you smile? You have to find the magic that will calm your anxiety and bring your focus back to the running. Then, you can slay your goals.

Chapter 8:

Beyond the Horizon: Exploring New Trails and Races

From Local Loops to International Trails: Embracing Diversity in Trail Running

One of the most exciting aspects of trail running is discovering new trails, races, events, and, of course, friends. As a novice, you will likely begin with an exploration of the venues available in your own backyard. My personal experience with this was an eye-opener, for sure. I knew about the popular local parks and hiking trails, and I had walked many of them over the years. When I began a more serious investigation into what was available, I was actually quite surprised! There were so many locations within a 30-minute drive—places I was previously unaware of. I researched local hikes, found a hiking location app, talked with a colleague who walked every weekend, and simply pored over maps. Within a month, I had identified five wonderful locations for trail running, all with unique features. I now had a repertoire of trails with varying lengths, altitudes, and degrees of difficulty right nearby. As I fell more and more in love with the trail, I also became increasingly curious about what was further afield. Finding a new trail was like finding a hidden treasure, and I soon found myself dedicating my weekend time to exploring hiking destinations further away. Not only have I discovered new trails since beginning my journey, but I've also visited new farmer's markets, restaurants, museums, boutiques, sports venues, and breweries! My neighborhood has expanded, and my world has opened up greatly.

I have a trail friend who actually plans his family vacations with running events in mind. When he schedules his time off, he works around races that he would like to enter and then trains for those accordingly. One of the beautiful consequences of this type of planning is that his partner and their children travel with him to locations they would otherwise not have chosen, many of which are national parks and backcountry paradises. While their schoolmates boast of trips to Legoland, his children regale their classmates with tales of exotic adventure, camping under the stars, hiking through forests, and hunting for wild blackberries.

Race Day Readiness

Your first trail race is so exciting, but also so intimidating and terrifying! Imagine you have read everything there is to read about the sport. You've worked with a club or coach to prepare. You've collected the gear, you've trained for months, and you've read the pre-race information packet so many times you have it memorized. You even carb-loaded with a lovely pasta dinner last night. Here you are at 6:00 am, race bib attached, waiting with the crowd of fidgety competitors for the start signal! And now you have to use the restroom!

No matter how well you've prepared for this day, you'll encounter surprises. So, one of the very best ways to prepare is to expect them. Trust that you have done your homework.

Trust that your body is strong and ready; after all, you've built up your endurance for months! Trust your fellow racers and event volunteers. They are there to cheer you on and ensure your safety.

Race day is like any other athletic or artistic performance. You will have nerves, but once you are actually in the moment, all that practice will pay off. Enjoy the experience and learn from it so you can tackle your next challenge with even more confidence, and don't forget to celebrate. Your first race is an enormous accomplishment!

Global Trail Destinations

At this point in my life, ultra running has taken me to seven different states, and that is just the beginning. I plan to continue to add to that count and see as much of the world as I can through the looking glass of trail running. I would never have known how beautiful Duluth, Minnesota, was had it not been for ultra marathons; or that Bandera, Texas, is so technical, rocky, and hilly; or that Kansas is not actually flat. Each new place gives me a new perspective and a newfound respect for the beauty of this world we live in. Believe me. This sport is going to open up your world in so many delightful ways!

As you read more and more about trail running, you will inevitably get the bug for world trail travel. So many countries host incredible events: Australia, Spain, China, Canada, the UK, Italy, and Kenya! Your options are only limited by your budget and your free time. Just like my running friend, many runners, particularly ultras, determine their world travel plans based on their running goals. I think the most wonderful aspect of this is that they see the natural beauty of each country they visit, rather than just the traditional tourist highlights.

I've discovered that, for me, the best way to seek out international events is to visit the website of the International Trail Running Association (ITRA). ITRA is a non-profit organization whose mission is to promote safe trail running for all. The website includes a calendar of race events, statistics on international rankings, trail talks, news releases, and all the technical information a runner would want to know. Many countries have their own national organizations, too. In the US, the American Trail Running Association (ATRA) is the place to start.

Just scrolling through the websites of trail running organizations will inspire you and invite you to travel the world one race at a time!

Chapter 9:

Connecting With the Trail Running Community

Trail running is a solo sport, not a team sport, unless you are participating in a relay, which is a lot of fun! However, that doesn't mean that runners train and race alone. The most successful and fulfilled runners find joy and safety in becoming active members of a running community.

The Importance of Joining a Community

You might first begin trail running by experimenting on your own on a local hiking trail. As you really get involved in the sport, though, you will find friends and inspiration by sharing your experience with others. Runners are often drawn into the sport by friends who share the same passion, but there are also those of us who will need to seek out our running community more intentionally.

Even a beginner runner can really benefit from the support of a club or coach. Those with more experience can relay excellent tips about training schedules. Not only that, but having other people invested in your training puts healthy pressure on you and provides some cheerleading. You may not feel like getting up before sunrise on a Saturday morning for a club run, but once you are up and out, the social element of that community will keep you on track. I know many runners who have turned in early after a TGIF because the morning club run was looming! When you think about it, getting up early for a bit of exercise and camaraderie is so much better than staying out too late and sleeping away half the weekend. Coaches offer the same kind of support and often have very specific expertise. They will be well-versed in the local climate and weather conditions and familiar with ideal running locations. Many coaches offer online support and will craft a plan specific to your fitness level and goals. Better still is a coach who can observe your running style and advise you on how to improve your form. A beginner runner may not wish to invest in a coach, but those who become more serious and competitive often do, as they want to optimize their experience (and health and safety).

Local Clubs

One of my running friends relayed her experience to me. She was not entirely new to running, as she had run 10Ks and a marathon some years back. Now, though, she was re-entering the field, having taken time off to start a family. She was really excited about trying out trail running because she loved the outdoors. So, she did her research and discovered a club not too far from her home. Club members met together twice a week to run local trails, which worked for her, but at first, she was hesitant to join. She was new to the trail. She was not in ideal shape. She didn't know the ins and outs of the sport. Would she be able to keep up? Would she hold back the other runners? Would she be the oldest in the group? She felt like a middle schooler on the first day of school.

She needn't have worried. Yes, at first, she did run at a slower pace than the other club members, but they didn't care. Rather, they welcomed her warmly and supported her with knowledge, cheerleading, and friendship. Now, some of those folks are her closest, lifelong friends. It took some guts for her to join a group where she was the most inexperienced, but remember that trail racing is all about courage and humility. If you can brave the backcountry, you can do anything!

These groups have had the biggest impact on my running. I was once that brand new person in the group—introverted and worried that I would be seen as an outsider. I could not have been more wrong! Years ago, I showed up to a running group on my own, which was very out of character for me, but I wanted running friends and figured that was the best way to find one. That first night, joining this particular run club practically changed my whole life. I met friends that later became like family and not only helped me to grow in trail running, face my first ultras, and PR a marathon, but they also helped me through some of the most challenging years of my personal life, too. The friendships I have made through running are some of the strongest bonds I have outside of family.

Coaches

Many trail runners, especially as they become more competitive in the sport, choose to hire coaches. Coaches might have backgrounds in sports psychology, physiology, physical therapy, nutrition, strength training, or motivation. Ideally, they are, or have been, trail runners themselves. Some coaches work virtually, initially focusing on crafting a long-term, individualized training plan based on the runner's experience, fitness level, goals, and time constraints. Often, they meet online or by phone once a week to check in and discuss additional topics like nutrition plans, strength training, injury prevention, and advice about form.

Other coaches meet with their clients in person. In addition to creating a training plan, they work closely to advise runners regarding their running form: posture, stride, foot strike, and coordination of arms and legs. This is much more effective with a live coach than online, but it depends on the local availability of coaches who match each runner's unique needs.

Even a runner who is not yet ready to compete seriously might benefit from a coach, particularly when it comes to correcting or improving running form right from the get-go. In the long run, a problematic form can cause overuse injuries, so having an expert analyze gait, stride, and foot strike can prevent issues later on. Coaching, of course, can be expensive, so for those who wish to keep the cost down, joining a running club might be a preferable first step.

For me, I have a coach who just so happens to be one of my best friends. The accountability is what draws me in. I'm not competing to win or training to be a professional athlete, but I love the accountability my coach provides. It makes it easier to get up in the morning or get a longer run in after work, knowing that someone took time out of their busy schedule to sculpt a plan just for me, as well as the reminder that I paid for this, so I might as well get the most out of it. Finding a coach will also help you get out of your comfort zone. I hate speed work and hill repeats, so if my training plan were up to me, I can assure you those two elements would not be a part of it. But they are important aspects of trail training and make me stronger in the long run.

Pacers

As runners participate in longer and more rigorous races, they may choose to work with a pacer. Some runners even act as pacers as they train for their own competitions in order to gain experience on a variety of trails and with different events. A pacer is a support person who runs alongside the competitor, cheerleading, helping to navigate, and watching the runner's health and safety. This heroic sidekick might remind the runner of the need for a nutrition or hydration break and will be on the lookout for fatigue or disorientation. Often, pacers join their runners somewhere along the route rather than right at the beginning, and it is typical for several pacers to take turns with a single runner, especially during an ultra. Pacers must be able to keep up with the trail runner over long distances. The last thing a competitor needs is a pacer who is holding up the process. On the other hand, when a runner's energy is flagging, the pacer must find the balance between slowing down to the runner's pace and encouraging the runner to get past the Pain Cave!

Although pacers are much more common in ultras, even beginner runners sometimes use pacers. These can even be running buddies from their local clubs who help them learn the dynamics of racing and act to push them forward.

Crew

While a crew is a must for an ultra runner, it can be a lovely addition even for a new trail runner. Your crew is essentially those wonderful friends and family members, or running colleagues, who assist you with your racing needs. They might be the folks who drive you to the starting line, the ones who await you at the finish and celebrate when they see you crossing, or those along the route who hand you water or snacks.

One of the ways to familiarize yourself with racing protocol before you decide to actually enter an event is to participate as a crew member for someone else. This is also a great way to stay connected to your running community if you have to take a break due to injury or recovery needs.

I swore I could never run 50 miles. Then, I crewed my friend on her first 50-miler. Watching her cross that finish line and seeing the sheer level of pride she had in that accomplishment made me want to do it. So, a year later, I ran in that same race I crewed her on, and I completed my first 50-miler. Crewing is hard. It may seem small to someone who does not understand all that goes into it, but knowing that someone is depending on you fully to succeed in their life-changing goals can be stressful and challenging. Getting to each aid station, having everything ready for your runner when they arrive (whether that be a change of clothes, shoes, food, or hydration), and just being there to encourage them to push forward is a lot of work, but so very rewarding. I love to watch my friends achieve ambitious goals, and there is pride in knowing that, in some small way, I helped get them there. Similarly, I am forever indebted to the friends and family that have crewed for me. These people have taken full weekends to follow me around in the woods and get me to my finish lines, and for that I am forever grateful. My son joined my crew a few years ago, and nothing made me happier than seeing him along the way and sharing my passion with him. Crewing is also a great way to involve your friends or family who may not be runners at all or not at the skill level of ultra running. I have had several friends crew me for races, and all of them have told me it was an incredible experience. To see the level of effort a runner pushes through and all that goes into these longer-distance races can inspire someone who is not engrossed in the ultra world to further appreciate the sport and even motivate them to get into trail running.

Technology-Based Communities

Online Forums

Online forums are a great way to connect with other trail runners. The conversational style of a virtual community lends itself to the efficient sharing of information, sometimes on very specific threads. In a forum, you'll be able to connect with runners from all over the world, not just with your local community. As with any form of social media, practice good digital citizenship and stay safe.

Social Media Platforms

There is an enormous amount to be learned just by following the social media posts of other runners. Maybe because they are so fanatical about their sport, trail runners love to post photos and stories about their runs. Their personal anecdotes can teach you everything from training tips to how to overcome mental obstacles, and from gear recommendations to the best events to join.

Digital Media

If you haven't joined your local library, get to it! Many trail running organizations produce online periodicals that highlight race stories, gear reviews, fitness and nutrition tips, and even recipes. Most libraries are free to join and offer digital access to e-books, audiobooks, and periodicals. I have excellent, free access to a variety of digital trail running magazines without actually having to travel to the library.

Podcasts

You will also want to explore podcasts. Although it's not recommended to have your earbuds in while you are on the trail or in traffic, you might use them on the treadmill or play a podcast in your car while commuting home from work. Again, there is a wealth of information and inspiring stories published by running organizations available in podcast form.

Trail Running Events

Group Runs

One of the most fun kinds of training is a local group run. They can be hosted by an organized club or simply serendipitously by fellow trail runners. Often, you will see announcements for organized local runs with a theme: color runs, pajama runs, night light runs, costume runs, or holiday runs. Group runs can be road or trail runs, or even a combination of both. Usually, organizers charge a registration fee and donate profits to charitable causes. Joining one of these runs is not only a fun time, but also pays back to your community. Runs that support environmental causes tend to be of particular interest to trail runners.

Workshops

Many athletic stores, running organizations, parks, and community centers offer workshops on hiking, the outdoors, or other elements connected to trail running. You might find a session on footwear, injury prevention, or orienteering. It's always a good idea to be on the lookout for classes in first aid and CPR; you never know when you might need to render aid to a fellow runner. You might also look at the offerings of extended learning programs on college campuses and adult education venues. Remember that workshops can be online as well as in person, so keep your eyes open.

Camps and Retreats

Running camps and retreats are a wonderful way to learn more about the sport. These are hosted all around the world in some really incredible locations, including world heritage sites. They focus on themes like wellness, mindfulness, or even culinary classes. Camps and retreats can range from roughing it under canvas to luxury accommodations with spa options. In addition to the actual trail running activities, many also offer sessions on yoga, wildlife viewing, local culture, or meditation. Depending on the location, nature of the accommodation, and length of stay, these can be pricey but offer a great way to destress or vacation!

The Importance of a Supportive Network

Regardless of whether you are connected to a local, regional, national, or international running community, or maybe all of the above, you will greatly benefit from belonging to a supportive group of like-minded athletes. Your trail running peers will swamp you with knowledge, inspire you, sweat, laugh and cry with you, pick you up when you stumble, and celebrate your successes with you. Maybe, more importantly, you will do the same for them.

Chapter 10:

The Trail Runner's Journey:

Growth, Transformation and

Joy

I hated running in high school, and if you had asked us to bet on which person in my friend group would become a runner later in life, no one would have guessed me. I was the person who walked and complained during the mile run at school. Then, I got a new officemate at work who told me he lost 40 pounds running a half marathon. I thought to myself, having just had my son, that I could run. I started out barely able to run 0.25 miles without walking and slowly inched my way a little farther each time. My first race was a five-mile race that I barely finished. Then a friend reached out to me, asking if I wanted to train for a half marathon, and I couldn't believe that people actually ran 13.1 miles for fun. I hesitantly agreed to it, and we trained up and finished the half marathon. That was when I got the bug. I then signed up for a marathon and completed that with the help of a coach through Team in Training: Endurance Events to End Cancer, organized through the Leukemia and Lymphoma Society. This was an incredible experience, and I knew I loved running, but it wasn't until about five years later that I would learn about trail running and the idea of running farther than a marathon. The next hurdle was a 50K, and I remember openly telling all my friends I was going to do one 50K, and that was it—there was no way I would ever run farther than that. I ran two 50Ks back-to-back and was pretty happy with knowing that I'd done it. But that little bug kept creeping back in. I then crewed a friend on a 50-miler and knew the bug wasn't going to go away, so I signed up for a 50-miler, but again swore I would never go any further than that. Then, I signed up for a 100K race (62.12 miles)! And although I have said I could never run 100 miles, even THAT bug is starting to creep in now.

Trail Wisdom

Mankind has been running through the wilderness since time began. In our modern world, however, it is all too easy to become distanced from the natural world and restricted to an urban life surrounded by concrete and smog. The wisdom we can gain from returning to our roots in nature is inestimable. Being at one with our own body and mind and with the wildlife and vegetation of the backcountry changes us—changes us for the better.

Perhaps the power of the trail is that it cleanses us. The trail compels us to leave our stress and angst behind for a while. It forces us to see ourselves with a clearer perspective, in our true place in the world, as beautiful, strong children of nature.

Life Lessons From the Trail

The trail teaches us so many lessons. It stretches our physical limits to extremes, helping us to recognize our body's incredible strength, endurance, and healing powers. Running in a wide variety of terrains and conditions shows us how flexible and responsive our bodies can be. Training for the trail entails studying nutrition, hydration, recovery strategies, and the mechanics of the human body.

When it comes to our character, running the trail delivers many precious gifts—gifts that will endure long after our running days have reached their peak: courage, resilience, tenacity, humility, patience, and even good humor. We experience success and failure and learn to value them equally. From this sport, we can learn wellness techniques and how to cultivate a state of flow.

Trail running also teaches us the core value that can change the world for the better: compassion. We practice compassion for ourselves as we learn to adapt our training to better care for our physical and mental health. We certainly practice compassion for our fellow runners, but I have also begun to feel a deeper sense of compassion for those with special needs who may not have the privilege of experiencing the joy of the trail as I do. Finally, there is no doubt that as we immerse ourselves more deeply in the natural environment, our compassion for all living things grows exponentially. It is not possible to embrace a life on the trail without learning to appreciate the animal and plant life that coexist in our space.

Continuing the Journey

You may decide to begin your adventure with an exploration of local hiking destinations. Then, you may choose to run your first 5K race. Once you are hooked, you will move on to 10Ks, half-marathons, and marathons. You might even continue your road racing, or you might devote yourself entirely to the trail. Do not be surprised if you start filling your weekend with club runs, find yourself reading about training camps, begin registering for trail racing retreats, and then plan your life around international ultra races. No matter what your unique journey is, it will impact every aspect of your life.

I promise that once you have hit the trail, there is no turning back. It's a point-to-point route, not an out-and-back! You will be hooked. addicted to the physical, mental, and spiritual energy you have learned to love.

Embracing the Trail Ahead

By now, you likely have a solid understanding of the intricacies of trail running. You have learned about gear, safety, physical training, emotional resilience, and all the wonderful benefits of this fabulous sport. I imagine you cannot wait to hit the trail! As you do, no doubt you will continue to learn about the amazing accomplishments you are capable of. I hope this introduction to trail running has provided you with the information and inspiration you need to jump right in!

Encouragement

The title of this book is not a coincidence. I truly believe that anyone can be a runner – even an ultra runner. I was inspired to write this book, because do not see myself as a natural born runner, it doesn't come easy to me, and I am continually working hard to achieve these goals. But I love it and I thought it important for others to hear the experiences, lessons, and perspective from someone who is just out to finish the race and do the best I can do without comparison to others. There is an ultra runner inside of all of us, if you want it, you're going to have to unleash it. And when you do the rewards and joy you will gain not only on the trail, but in your personal life and chasing your dreams are endless. When you are tired or feeling defeated, always remember what you have learned here. Take a breath, dig in your heels, and look ahead, not down. There is no end to what you can achieve.

Conquering Your Fears

Many trail runners have real fears when they first embrace their new challenge. Will I be sufficiently fit? Will I injure myself? What if I don't understand the rules of the race? Will I get lost? Will I make an idiot of myself? What if I cross the finish line last? If we think back to our earliest experiences, we are always a bit afraid of something new. Soon, however, the courage kicks in, and we begin to see the promise of adventure. So, maybe answer all these questions with the worst-case scenario. You may not be perfectly fit at first, but you will get there. If you don't understand all the rules of the race, someone will undoubtedly show you. If you get lost, prepare ahead of time to figure out how to get found again! If you are the last to cross the finish line, good for you! Celebrate your tenacity!

Something that I have found so endearing about the trail running community is that even the best runners in the world are always willing to help out and encourage their fellow runners. I have run with athletes that far exceeded my skills and speed and have found it so powerful to have them running next to me, telling me I am doing great or look strong. This community is amazing. It's ok to have fears and be nervous about something new, but I can assure you that the trail running community is ready to embrace you.

Final Thoughts

Your Trail Running Story

Painters collect their work in portfolios. Writers hoard hundreds of old notebooks. Scientists cannot function without lab reports. Professional cooks and bakers make notes on their recipes. As you begin trail running or as you transition from road to trail, take the time to journal about your experiences. Write down your goals. Note the details of your runs: date, time, weather, speed, terrain, and how you felt. Add photos if you like. Record details of your strength workouts: weights, repetitions, and machines or dumbbells. Add comments about nutrition and hydration. What are you learning about your body's need for fuel? Describe the beauty of the natural environments you visit, and dream about the new trails you'd like to explore. What about the new friends you meet in the process? What are you learning from them and about them? More importantly, what are you learning about yourself? Congratulate yourself for the incremental wins. Jot down stories about the challenges, disappointments, and joys of your runs. You will notice that in the first three to six months of your new sport, you will see a beautiful story emerge. Then, be sure to share your story with others. You will be a true inspiration!

Trail running has changed my life in so many ways over the last several years. Not only have I done things I never thought possible, but I have also found a community along the way that is supportive, healthy, and strong. There is a whole new world just waiting to be explored, and I look forward to all this journey has in store for you.

Sarah Russell's Unleashing Your Inner Ultrarunner

Review Request Page

Thank you so much for taking the time to read this book. I hope it has given you the knowledge and inspiration needed to begin or continue your ultrarunning journey. May this book be the inspiration you needed to enjoy the magic of trail running and conquering ultramarathons.

Now that you have finished the book, I want to ask if you would share your thoughts by writing a review. Your review on this book could be the light at the end of the trail for someone else just starting out. It costs nothing and takes less than a minute, but it could make a huge difference in someone's ultrarunning journey.

Simply click the link or scan the QR code to leave your review:

Your act of kindness can change lives and dreams. Thank you from the depths of my heart for being part of this journey.

Looking forward to sharing more exciting adventures and running strategies in the future. Happy Trails!

Best wishes,
Sarah Russell

References

Achilles International. (n.d.). Achilles International. http://achillesinternational.org

Bolt, R. (2018, May 31). *National Directory of Trail Work Organizations.* ATRA. https://trailrunner.com/trail-news/national-directory-of-trail-work-organizations/

Borg, G. (1998). *APA PsycNet.* Psycnet.apa.org. https://psycnet.apa.org/record/1998-07179-000

Craggs, T. (2021, May 7). *What is a fartlek run and how can it help you get faster?* Runner's World. https://www.runnersworld.com/uk/training/a36362823/fartlek-run/

Csikszentmihalyi, M. (1990). *Flow: The Psychology of Optimal Experience.* Goodreads. https://www.goodreads.com/book/show/66354.Flow

Dan, B. (2015). *History of Blue Zones - Blue Zones.* Blue Zones. https://www.bluezones.com/about/history/

Eidel, S. (2022, July 5). *Runner's Diet.* Www.hopkinsmedicine.org. https://www.hopkinsmedicine.org/health/wellness-and-prevention/runners-diet

Food and Nutrition Information Center (FNIC) | National Agricultural Library. (n.d.). Www.nal.usda.gov. https://www.nal.usda.gov/programs/fnic

Kluwer, W. (2021). *Physical Activity Guidelines Resources.* ACSM_CMS. https://www.acsm.org/education-resources/trending-topics-resources/physical-activity-guidelines/lists/guidelines-resources/physical-activity-guidelines-for-americans-2nd-edition#:~:text=All%20healthy%20adults%20aged%2018

MacBride-Stewart, S. (2019). Discourses of wellbeing and environmental impact of trail runners in protected areas in New Zealand and the United Kingdom. *Geoforum, 107,* 134–142. https://doi.org/10.1016/j.geoforum.2019.09.015

Poets' Corner - Bliss Carman - The Joys of the Road. (n.d.). Www.theotherpages.org. https://www.theotherpages.org/poems/2001/carman0102.html

Staurowsky, E. J., Desouza, M. J., Ducher, G., Gentler, N., Miller, K. E., Shakib, S., Theberge, N., & Williams, N. (2009). *Her Life Depends On It II Sport, Physical Activity, and the Health and Well-Being of American Girls and Women.* https://files.eric.ed.gov/fulltext/ED515841.pdf

Team In Training: Endurance Events To End Cancer | Leukemia and Lymphoma Society. (n.d.). Www.lls.org. Retrieved October 10, 2023, from https://www.lls.org/article/team-training-endurance-events-end-cancer

Terry Fox Foundation. (2021). *Terry's Story - The Terry Fox Foundation.* The Terry Fox Foundation. https://terryfox.org/terrys-story/

Trail Ultra Project. (n.d.). Trail Ultra Project. Retrieved October 9, 2023, from http://www.trailultraproject.com

Printed in Great Britain
by Amazon